THE PRAC

Marilyn Cochran-

(continued)

IMPACTFUL PRACTITIONER INQUIRY

THE RIPPLE EFFECT ON CLASSROOMS, SCHOOLS, AND TEACHER PROFESSIONALISM

Sue Nichols
Phil Cormack

TEACHERS COLLEGE PRESS

TEACHERS COLLEGE | COLUMBIA UNIVERSITY

NEW YORK AND LONDON

Published by Teachers College Press, 1234 Amsterdam Avenue, New York, NY
10027

Library of Congress Cataloging-in-Publication Data is available at loc.gov

ISBN 978-0-8077-5672-0 (paper)
ISBN 978-0-8077-7390-1 (ebook)

Printed on acid-free paper
Manufactured in the United States of America

23 22 21 20 19 18 17 16   8 7 6 5 4 3 2 1

Contents

CHAPTER 1

Practitioner Inquiry
What's the Impact?

Teacher research "may be difficult to implement." This was the cautious statement made in 1978, when the Bay Area Writing Project had just embarked on a first wave of practitioner research collaborations (Gray & Myers, 1978, p. 413). A decade later, reports were coming through about the transformations experienced by teachers when they engaged in classroom-based research. Among these transformations were that teachers "step up their use of resources; they form networks; and they become more active professionally" (Goswami & Stillman, 1987, p. ii). In 1999, Cochran-Smith and Lytle (1999) published a retrospective on the practitioner inquiry movement in which they argued that "the concept of teacher research carries with it an enlarged view of the teacher's role—as decision maker, consultant, curriculum developer, analyst, activist, school leader—as well as enhanced understandings of the contexts of educational change" (p. 17). That same year, the "knowledge-creating school" was being advanced as a model for educational renewal that was clearly influenced by the kind of inquiring professionalism that the teacher research movement had been advocating (Hargreaves, 1999).

More than a decade on, we feel it is important to continue making such arguments. Indeed, it has been humbling to us to gain a renewed appreciation for the innovative and groundbreaking work of the stalwarts of teacher research (Altrichter, Posch, & Somekh, 1993; Elliott, 1978; Freeman, 1998; Kemmis, 2006; Lytle & Cochran-Smith, 1992; Noffke & Stevenson, 1995). We are also very mindful of the foundational thinking of pioneers such as Berthoff (1981), Stenhouse (1985), and Schön (1983). All these thinkers and doers have been influential on our own work as inquiring practitioners and supporters of practitioner inquiry.

It was as inquiring practitioners that we initiated the Impacts of Practitioner Inquiry (IPI) project in 2008. The University of South Australia had been for some time a hub for passionate teacher educators, drawn from schools, who had integrated practitioner inquiry into a succession of graduate programs and collaborative research projects. We want to acknowledge these colleagues by name: Marie Brennan, Mike Chartres, Barbara Comber, Bill Green, Rob Hattam, Lyn Kerkham, David Lloyd, Helen Nixon, Kathy

Paige, Jo Reid, and Pat Thomson. Together, we had worked with many hundreds of teachers and school leaders to embed inquiry into professional practice and to attempt the complex work of acquiring the dual habitus of educator and researcher. We also want to acknowledge the many education departments and organizations that supported practitioner inquiry as part of their research agendas and, in particular, the Division of Education, Arts and Social Sciences at University of South Australia (UniSA) and the Senior Secondary Assessment Board of South Australia (now the SACE Board of SA) for providing funding to support the IPI project.

The context within which we embarked on the IPI investigation was one of debate about the value and purpose of any form of educational research not fitting into the "gold standard" of randomized controlled trials (Howe, 2009). Because qualitative and contextualized educational research was being excluded from the evidence base, teachers were being compelled to implement "evidence-based" practices, particularly in our field of expertise, literacy (Cunningham, 2001). It seemed there was no longer any need for teachers to ask questions; they were all being answered by science. Indeed, teachers' questions were seen as obstacles to their faithful following of the pedagogic scripts (Owens, 2010). We are currently seeing that large-scale reform efforts are reaching the limits of top-down accountability, and it is being accepted in some quarters that teachers' adaptation and modification of mandated programs might strengthen the programs' effectiveness (Lewis, 2015). However, the idea that teachers might pose their own questions or direct their own inquiries or that effectiveness might be judged by anything other than scores on standardized tests does not enter into these limited forms of teacher agency. At the outset, we declare our view that teacher agency, and particularly the right to pose questions, is at the heart of practitioner inquiry and, we will argue, the basis of its power to achieve change.

This book aims to continue and strengthen arguments for the validity and usefulness of practitioner inquiry by bringing together the key lessons we have learned from our involvement in such research over decades. We were especially keen to explore ways in which practitioner research is impactful—that is, how it can make a positive difference in sites of practice. To this end, we established a project to investigate the kinds of impacts inquiry can make and how and why practitioners believe it contributes to change. In the following section, we describe the project that provides the basis of the first section of the book.

THE IMPACTS OF THE PRACTITIONER INQUIRY PROJECT

The IPI project began by amassing a database of 339 educators who had participated in inquiry via programs in which we had been involved over the previous 10 years, either in a graduate program or as part of a collaborative project. Many of these individuals were no longer at their previous schools, which itself points to the mobile nature of the teaching workforce. In some cases, the trail went cold and we were unable to reach some teachers. We succeeded in contacting 290 educators.

Data collection for IPI had three components: a survey, interviews with practitioners, and interviews with nominated colleagues of practitioners. The survey (see the Appendix) had five sections:

A. Practitioner inquiry projects. Respondents identified up to five projects they had been involved in during the previous 10 years. Those involved in more than five projects were asked to choose the five they found most significant.

B. Inquiry practices. Respondents were invited to select from a list of common inquiry practices those they had employed in their inquiries; they could add additional practices if necessary.

C. Impacts. Respondents were asked to consider effects that their involvement in practitioner inquiry had on their professional practice and on their careers.

D. The most impactful projects. Respondents were asked to indicate which projects from those identified in Section A had been most significant in terms of their professional practice and career.

E. Further information. This section asked respondents to provide information on their current role, years in the profession, school level(s) they worked in, and participation in academic study involving practitioner inquiry. Finally, they were asked if they were willing to be interviewed.

Follow-up interviews with those who volunteered were designed to be generative rather than simply to provide descriptions of impact. Projects' direct and immediate impacts on practice are typically what most end-point evaluations of practitioner inquiry projects focus on. We were interested in both the immediate and enduring impacts of inquiry experiences. To this end, we designed the interview around topics and scenarios, rather than making it a series of questions. The idea of the topics was to engage practitioners in extended reflection around specific projects to get a sense of the contexts for practice they provided. The topics were the immediate impact of a particular project, a project that still lives with you, and inquiry-related career impacts.

Participants were also invited to respond to a number of scenarios designed to explore how their experience across a range of projects made them think about the potential impacts of practitioner inquiry in a more general way. The scenarios were:

- advising a colleague about potential involvement in a practitioner inquiry project;
- making a leadership decision about whether and how to involve staff in a practitioner inquiry project; and
- responding to a policy paper that includes practitioner inquiry skills as part of a set of required teacher competencies.

Further interviews with nominated colleagues/managers of the interviewees were sought both to triangulate and to provide an organizational perspective on the impacts of a particular educator's participation in inquiry. Colleagues were asked if they were able to recall a specific inquiry project that had an immediate or longer-term impact, to describe both the focus teacher's role and their own role, and to describe its impacts. They were also asked to express a view regarding the advantages and disadvantages to the organization of personnel being involved in practitioner inquiry.

THE IPI PARTICIPANTS AND THEIR INQUIRY PROJECTS

Of the 58 participants who responded to the IPI survey, most (44) had more than 15 years of teaching experience and were school based (40). Of the school-based educators, 25 were currently classroom teachers and the others were in leadership positions. The survey also included 18 practitioners located in district or head offices at the time of responding. Similar to the teaching population, the majority of respondents were female (76%).

Collectively, the group had undertaken 123 practitioner inquiry projects. Just under half had undertaken one inquiry and about a quarter had conducted two inquiries. The remainder had conducted three or more inquiries. However, as the survey findings showed, many practitioners integrated inquiry practices into their professional work, even if the integration did not take the form of specific projects.

Projects were generally 12 months in duration (46%), but some lasted up to 3 years. Most of the projects were undertaken as part of a group, either at the school level or in networks of multiple sites. Only 16% were solo inquiries. Many of the projects were undertaken in association with graduate studies, including those that were initiated by state education departments or other education systems. Over half of the respondents (36) received academic credit for at least one of their projects.

When participants were asked to nominate a project that had the most significant impact on practice, they ranked highest those that lasted 12 months or longer in duration and that were conducted in partnerships involving other practitioners beyond their schools. The survey also asked educators to describe the features of the nominated projects that they viewed as most impactful. Based on their comments, projects that produce impacts could be described in the following ways: These projects generated data that were more extensive and multilayered than what was typically available from day-to-day practice; they introduced theories and new knowledge; and they provided opportunities to apply theories and knowledge to practice, through interpretation of the data, in social contexts of peer dialogue. Sharing learning in the form of presentations or reports gave practitioners recognition and confidence and crystallized the knowledge gained.

Of the IPI survey informants, 30 educators agreed to be interviewed; of these, we were able to arrange interviews with 20. Difficulties with coordinating researcher and teacher time and in connecting with educators in remote and rural settings meant that not all willing teachers were able to be included. Because of the large demand for interviews with survey participants, we were able to conduct only a small number of interviews (five) with nominated colleagues/managers.

We acknowledge here the generosity of all the educators who participated in the IPI project through responding to the survey and/or making their valuable time available to us for interviews. For ethical reasons the project cannot use the real names of these educators or their students in this book, nor identify their work sites. All names of practitioners and students used in this book are pseudonyms with a few exceptions. In some cases, where not bound by institutional ethics conditions, educators gave us permission to include direct quotations from their work (published material or unpublished reports from university work) and requested that their real names be used— where this is the case, the educators' work is included in the references.

THE AUTHORS AS INQUIRING PRACTITIONERS

In the field of educational research, distinctions are often made between researchers and practitioners. In our cases, we began our professional careers as school-based educators, and began to develop as inquirers within these practice settings. We were fortunate enough to be trained and work during the time and place in which the late Garth Boomer was arguing strongly about the importance of teachers and students being inquirers (Boomer, 1985; Boomer, Lester, Onore, & Cook, 1992). Boomer (1985) could not bear the idea of mechanistic education. He sketched a gloomy scenario:

> Imagine education-department curriculum guides, with no explicit learning theory, being taken by teachers with no explicit learning theory and turned into lessons for children who are not told the learning theory. (p. 5)

Imagine! It is not too hard even decades later. Boomer argued that if students were to become inquiring learners, teachers had to become informed and inquiring educators (Comber, 2013). Significantly, Boomer (1985) included universities and schools within a single vision for inquiry-oriented educational practice:

> Since schools and universities are institutions for the promotion of deliberate learning, all teaching . . . should be directed towards the support of deliberate, personally owned and conducted, solution-oriented investigation. All teachers should be experts in "action research" so that they can show students how to be "action researchers." (p. 125)

We came into the academy with this habitus already in the process of developing and have been able to continue our growth as inquiring educators in a university setting. Working with colleagues from school, early childhood, and adult education has deepened our understanding of practice in these areas.

Working toward this book has been a process of reflecting on and analyzing our own practice as supporters, facilitators, and collaborators in research involving practitioners as inquirers. Teachers are great archivists and have elephantine memories for the people, activities, and moments that inspired or depressed them. This explains how we have come to amass considerable personal libraries and museums of artifacts of our practice. In working through these materials, we have generated questions to guide our self-reflective inquiry:

- What were our intentions in designing inquiries and inquiring strategies in particular ways?
- What do we know about how educators experienced these inquiry activities?
- What theories underpinned our practice then and our analysis now?
- What tensions or contradictions were being negotiated in the course of these inquiries and activities?
- How was difference being managed in the process of undertaking these inquiries?
- What do we consider evidence of impact of our own practices as supporters of practitioner inquiry?

The phrase "opening the black box" was suggested at one point to describe this process and our motivation. However, it would be misleading to suggest that the "contents" of such a "box" are simply there to be viewed once the lid has been removed. To stretch the metaphor a little, it was evident from our discussions that neither of us would have the same box or contents as the other. We accepted that this process would be one of assembling, interpreting, and coauthoring an account from diverse materials drawn from our respective histories of practice.

OVERVIEW OF THE BOOK

Part I reports the findings of the IPI project in three chapters, focusing on impacts on professional practice, school cultures, and career trajectories, respectively. In Part II, the experiences of the IPI teachers and our own combine to form the basis for an exploration of two specific inquiry projects. In this section, we examine two projects that were nominated by some of the IPI teachers as among "the most impactful" and in which we participated in various roles: as facilitators, co-researchers, and graduate program coordinators. Part III focuses on what we see as two important but relatively underexamined aspects of the practitioner inquiry process: design and analysis. Here, we describe specific practices that are integral to developing impactful inquiries, based not only on the experiences of the IPI cohort but on effective practices developed across many projects. To develop this account, we have been engaged in a process of artifact collection, documentation, reflection, and critical analysis.

As we draw these threads together in the concluding chapter, we will discuss four overarching themes. First, the effectiveness of practitioner inquiry is integrally connected to teachers' sense of accountability, which is strongly activated by a desire to improve the learning experiences of students most at risk. This challenges the view of teachers as needing the external discipline of regulatory powers in order to force them to assume accountability for student learning outcomes. Second, impactful practitioner inquiry is as much conceptual as it is practical. Educators find inquiries impactful when they challenge themselves to think and speak differently about their practice, their students, the curriculum, and the nature of teaching and learning. This conceptual work is driven by divergence, debate, and dialogue much more so than consensus. Third, the unpredictable and dynamic impacts of inquiring practitioners in the classroom, school, and profession are much better explained by networking and complexity models than linear hierarchical models. Fourth, practitioner inquiry aligns well with new models of teacher and curriculum leadership in maintaining a central focus on the practice of teaching while building skills of design, analysis, communication, collaboration, and networking. To conclude, we discuss debates about the relative characteristics of academic and practitioner research and argue that a view of research as disengaged and decontextualized not only disqualifies practitioner inquiry but impoverishes educational research in general.

PART I

IMPACTS OF PRACTITIONER INQUIRY

CHAPTER 2

Impacts in the Classroom and Other Sites of Practice

"Since I did the practitioner inquiry it's been a real passion"

To understand the impact of practitioner inquiry on professional practice, particularly over a teacher's career, it is necessary to understand the complexities of practice. Professional practice is always enacted in context. These contexts include aspects that are more, and also less, within the control of participants, including curriculum frameworks, spatial architecture, resources, histories, and personalities. Kemmis (2009) refers to these elements of context as "mediating preconditions [that] structure how [practice] unfolds in words and discourses . . . in action and interaction in physical and material space-time" (pp. 22–23). Teachers' understanding of these conditions is thus vital in their decisions about how to practice their profession. Over the course of a career, educators often move between contexts, a process that requires continual learning and adjustment. Even moving from a Grade 2 class to a Grade 4 class in the same school brings with it different curriculum, developmental level, physical environment, and collegial relationships.

Educational practice can be understood as bringing together judgment and action and, as a result, it is full of ethical challenges. Teaching has been described as a practice of human improvement that aims to transform lives (Cohen, 2005). It carries significant risks of failing to change what needs to be changed and of potentially worsening the situation for some learners (Le Fevre, 2014). In attempting to minimize these risks, educators may prefer to maintain practices that work sufficiently well for the majority of students (Attard, 2007). Others are continually "haunted" (Green, 2009) by the knowledge that what works for the majority continues to let down other learners who deserve better.

Educators make judgments in the moment, taking into account what they know about learning in general, about learning in a particular subject area, and about a particular group of learners. In this process, teachers put "into practice" what they know and simultaneously learn from their students about the relevance of their knowledge to the particular problem at hand (Taylor, 2015). Teachers as a profession are often characterized as tinkerers (Huberman, 1993), disposed to trying out activities and always interested in new "tips and tricks." However, the decision to integrate an approach into the practice repertoire is a serious one. A teacher's "arsenal" (Everitt, 2012) is assembled over time and consists of strategies the teacher has found reliable as well as adaptable to specific classes and individual learners.

It should also be noted that there are many practice roles available in the education field. The practice of a full-time educational leader is not the same as that of a full-time classroom practitioner. The leadership practice of a kindergarten director is not the same as that of a high school principal or a head office administrator. A school librarian's practice is very different from a counselor's. Educators may combine roles such as leadership and classroom teaching, and they may move between roles over a career (see Chapter 4).

It is in this complex context that we consider how practitioner inquiry has come into productive connection with the practice of educating, in all its forms. Inquiry has power to the extent that it can act in the service of educational practice. Though we disagree with the proposition that teachers cannot be "real"' researchers (see Chapter 9), it is true that educational research is not always directly in the service of practice (Noffke, 2008). Educators who are invited to take up inquiry will put it to the test of relevance.

In this chapter, we describe ways in which practitioners have found inquiry to be relevant and compelling in helping them improve their practice. First, inquiry practices such as reflection, reading, and discussion enabled teachers to gain distance on their practice and consider ways of interrupting business as usual. As part of this, teachers often shifted from deficit- to strength-based perspectives on their students. Second, gaining experience in designing and undertaking inquiries encouraged teachers to bring inquiry learning into their classrooms. Third, trialing innovations on practice assisted teachers to make decisions about expanding their practice repertoire.

Teachers' ethical commitments and practical judgment mediated their judgments of their inquiries. They judged inquiries as impactful not just when those inquiries enabled the teacher to take up a new practice, but even more important, when doing so made a genuine difference to students. Connected to this, teachers were particularly alert to the impact of interventions on the students of most concern—that is, those who most often were seen in deficit terms, as failing or disengaged. When the evidence showed that a particular strategy was successful with the most problematic or least-achieving students, the strategy was rated highly and was added to the teacher's repertoire.

THE IPI SURVEY

The IPI survey asked educators about their inquiry practices and about what they believed to be the impacts of inquiry on their professional practice. Inquiry can be understood as a set or repertoire of practices, assembled in different ways by inquiring individuals and teams. We first wanted to find out which practices characterized the inquiries undertaken by the educators.

Design is a significant element in inquiry (see Chapter 7), concerned with what is to be investigated, why, and how. Whether a topic is imposed by system priorities or whether it arises from an individual concern can make a difference to whether and how a teacher subsequently integrates learning from the inquiry into her practice. Figure 2.1 shows teachers' responses to various inquiry design options that were provided in the survey.

In the project design stage, the most common practice was engaging in academic/professional reading, selected by nearly three-quarters of respondents (42). Almost as many (39) indicated that their experience as a practitioner contributed significantly to the project design. Thus, project development drew on both scholarly and professional knowledge. Most of these educators had a strong element of personal agency in the design of their projects through developing their own research questions (39) and making their own decisions about data collection (35).

Next, we were interested in how the educators generated evidence to inform their analyses and address their inquiry questions. The teachers' responses to the survey indicated that inquiry practices both drew from and added to teachers' regular professional practices. For instance, collecting student assignments, keeping a journal, and examining institutional records

Figure 2.1. Design Practices in Practitioner Inquiries (*n* = 58; *r* = 242)

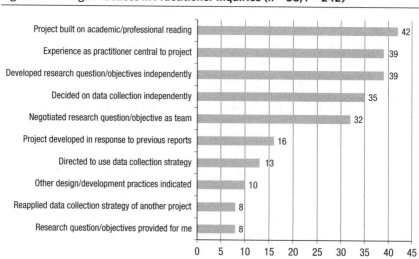

are ordinary activities for educators, whereas designing surveys, interviewing, and undertaking case studies are more often considered research activities. Thus, there was not a strict separation of inquiry and educational practices; rather, educators' inquiry repertoires were extended by their teaching repertoires and vice versa. The top-ranked inquiry practice was observing students (42). We argue that making a difference to students was both a major motivating factor for educators undertaking inquiry and the litmus test of success. Therefore, it makes sense that observing students was a favored inquiry strategy.

In terms of impacts of practitioner inquiry on practice, the most often reported educator impacts were the following:

1. Viewed the curriculum differently (45)
2. Developed new resources (43)
3. Saw new connections between practice and theory (41)
4. Increased the diversity of learning activities (40)
5. Modified existing resources (38)
6. Viewed students differently (37)
7. Made more use of Information and Communication Technologies (ICTs) for learning (35)
8. Incorporated more opportunities for student choice (32)
9. Increased the range of assessment practices (30)
10. Integrated inquiry practices into teaching (30)

Across these responses, a number of themes can be identified. First, practitioner inquiry was associated with seeing aspects of one's practice, context, and students differently (1, 3, and 6). Second, as a result of undertaking inquiry, educators diversified their practices, creating a wider range of tasks, processes, and methods for evaluating learning (4, 8, and 9). Third, inquiring practitioners worked actively with resources, producing or modifying materials in order to create new kinds of learning opportunities (2, 5, and 7). Finally, educators incorporated inquiry into their pedagogy.

The practitioner interviews enabled us to further understand the connection between inquiry and its impacts on professional practice and praxis. In the remainder of the chapter, we discuss five aspects of this through the experiences of the interviewees. First, we explore the link between practitioner inquiry and new ways of seeing practice. Then, we look at examples of educators integrating inquiry into their teaching programs. Following this, we consider how teachers' ethical concerns are included, especially in terms of teachers' commitment to the students of most concern and the ways in which the teachers mobilized inquiry to address these concerns. We also consider how some educators transferred a case study approach from inquiry into their teaching and leadership. Finally, we briefly consider impacts on practices in roles other than classroom teaching and school leadership, with specific reference to the outcomes of a school counselor's inquiry.

SEEING WITH FRESH EYES

Before an educator can marshal the mental energy and commitment to change her practice, it is necessary to become aware of that practice as she is currently engaging in it. It has often been noted that awareness of practice in teaching operates on a tacit level, meaning it is rarely explicitly articulated unless there is a specific occasion for such articulation (Attard, 2007; Freeman, 1993; Nind & Thomas, 2005). As one teacher, Pat, explained, the relentless flow of daily events created a kind of forgetfulness, in which the original rationale for a practice became lost as it continued to be repeated without reflection:

> We tend to just keep going and just keep using, using what you've got and forgetting how you got it, or where it came from, and sort of not understanding that it was important. You kind of forget and you just keep thinking, "Oh well, that's done, over, let's move on to the next thing."

Even when educators were aware at some level that their practices were not always optimal, the dulling nature of routine meant they could drift away from their better selves. This risk was expressed by one teacher, Alessandra, as the fear of becoming "a crusty teacher who teaches from a textbook."

One of the most significant impacts of teachers' participation in inquiry was in interrupting the taken-for-granted flow of classroom life. We can see some links here with the kinds of inquiry practices identified above. It may be that the experience of seeing differently at least in part was owed to the use of observation as an inquiry method. Taking fieldnotes during or after an activity or producing audio or video records enabled teachers to stop the flow of practice. They could then focus on participants, interactions, and significant moments. In most cases, this was combined with one or more other methods of capturing learning events such as interviewing, artifact collection, or testing.

Penny described her experience as "putting the microscope over a piece of practice . . . you come out really clear about what you need to do to improve it." Ben experienced inquiry as a deconstructive and reorienting process that involved "getting your head around what you'd actually done and digesting it, and pulling it apart, and then sort of formalizing it." Both teachers' statements express a sense of the distancing that enables educators to examine their practice and imagine it differently, identifying missed opportunities and moments when leaps of learning occur.

One of the consequences of this forensic view was that classroom teachers gained insight into what it was like being a student in their class. Gemma described developing the habit of switching her orientation from teacher to learner:

> It was about repositioning myself from then on, to step out of your teacher headset and put on the learner role. And that's really different, but it's also been really important in terms of the way you ask yourself questions. And you become more, I became more open.

Inquiry created an interruption that shifted practitioners' standpoints, enabling a new view of business as usual. Coming to this new standpoint was experienced by some as a form of defamiliarization. For educational administrators, this might mean shaking off, at least temporarily, some of the bureaucratic frameworks that shaped their everyday practice. Natasha, a senior manager, spoke about having to "un-train" herself from habitual ways of writing and thinking, an experience that felt so transgressive that she described it humorously as "exploring on the dark side."

Shifts in perspective were particularly significant when they concerned students for whom deficit views had become entrenched. When, even with teachers' best efforts, students do not achieve, acceptance can set in as the student acquires an identity of "'disengaged," "disorganized," or "slow learner." In the next section, we discuss how these students became the sharpest tests of teachers' interventions and how inquiry enabled teachers to satisfy their own criteria of making a difference for those students who needed most support.

INTEGRATING INQUIRY LEARNING

When we examined the impacts of participation in practitioner inquiry on teachers' classroom practice, one of the most striking was in the integration of inquiry approaches. Many of the teachers had been familiar with the broad area of active learning and had used project, discovery, or design approaches in the past. Once they had taken on the identity of inquirers for themselves, two shifts were evident: First, there was a greater emphasis on questioning and openness as hallmarks of inquiry. Second, there was an increased focus on modeling as a key pedagogic strategy.

Inquiry-based learning is increasingly becoming a requirement in school curricula, particularly in science, mathematics, and technology (Marshall, Horton, Igo, & Switzer, 2009; Ramnarain, 2013). Proponents link inquiry learning methods to deeper understanding of concepts and a stronger appreciation for the relevance of academic knowledge for solving real-world problems. Advocating for this approach, Bybee (2006) writes:

> If students are truly to understand science and develop useful skills, they cannot simply read, memorize, and recite isolated bits of information and vocabulary words. They must take time to wrestle with new ideas, to discuss their ideas with their classmates and teachers, to collect data and use it to draw conclusions, to practice skills, and finally relate what they are learning to the world around them. (p. 8)

However, efforts to encourage the integration of inquiry learning have met with only "modest success" (DeBoer, 2006, p. 21). As with many reform efforts, teachers have been blamed for the lack of successful and widespread uptake. Educators have been accused of taking a superficial approach in which hands-on or activity learning is substituted for authentic problem-focused investigation (DeBoer, 2006). Teachers' discomfort with inquiry learning is associated with a belief that "[r]esearch is something that researchers do" (Abell, Smith, & Volkmann, 2006, p. 192).

One outcome of practitioner inquiry is that the practice of research becomes something that educators do. The IPI teachers saw themselves as inquirers. Thus, they were less likely simply to tell students *what* to do and more able to show them *how*. Dean taught Legal Studies to senior secondary students. As with many courses at this level, students are required to select a topic and conduct an independent project as a major assessment component. Dean reported that many of his colleagues found this element difficult to teach, especially in helping students design a focus question for their inquiry.

Curriculum frameworks tend to depict research processes as linear, progressing neatly from the initial question through data collection to analysis and conclusions (Dudu & Vhurumuku, 2012). Striking among the experienced teacher researchers was the nuanced and engaged character they brought to inquiry-based learning in their classes. Melanie explained the difference she saw between standard classroom inquiry and what she called "real inquiry":

> [T]eachers might think they're doing an inquiry because they're giving choice, but in actual fact you already know what the expected outcome is going to be. . . . *Real* inquiry is very open. You're always open to which·path, there's not a specific [outcome]. So lateral thinking comes out of it, which you don't get if you've already got an end product in mind.

Melanie described how she used her understanding of inquiry when leading her students in an environmental studies investigation focused on coming up with solutions to the problem of water wastage. She modeled openness and in so doing facilitated the emergence of innovative environmental solutions from her students. While she explicitly taught a set of skills that included data analysis and reporting, she also made room for creative and critical thinking. This, in her view, made the crucial distinction between ordinary projects and *real* inquiry. Melanie's students went beyond obvious solutions to advance possibilities she had not predicted:

> Most people, if you asked: "What are you going to use gray [waste] water for?" [would say] "I'll water the vegetable garden, fill up the swimming pool, water the lawn." But kids come up with different ways to approach it. . . . They decided they were going to use the gray water to put around the perimeter of the house to stop the houses from cracking in the hot weather. You give them scope to allow them to think, which allows people to go really divergent and come up with creative ideas.

When teachers remain entrenched in the "knower" identity, students are encouraged to believe that the answer to any question already resides in the teacher. This provides little incentive for students to take the risk of embarking on a process of discovery with an uncertain outcome. When teachers take on an inquiry orientation, it appears that their students correspondingly develop more independent learner identities (Oppong-Nuako, Shore, Saunders-Stewart, & Gyles, 2015). Experiencing inquiry for themselves helps teachers become more at ease with shifting between "knower" and "learner" identities. Joan described her shift as a "turnaround moment," at which point she realized, "just because I don't have the knowledge myself doesn't mean that I can't facilitate [my students'] exploring." Joan's students not only undertook inquiries but also presented their findings in a public forum attended by professional engineers. When audience members insisted on referring to Joan as the authority, she stood aside to allow her students to display their knowledge:

> I put it together but they talked about their individual projects and what the learning had meant for them. And there was a technical question and I said "I don't know, I'm just a deputy, ask them." And that was, I think, a really big aha moment for those guys, too, the engineers.

Gemma used an inquiry approach to engage her students in thinking about learning, and more broadly, the social purpose of education. As the coordinator of services for students with learning difficulties, she was responsible for engaging the students in goal setting, monitoring progress, and designing curriculum options. She decided to develop a course, creditable toward the senior certificate [high school diploma], titled Students as Researchers. In explaining the approach taken in this course, Gemma compared it to other courses with research requirements:

> In History they identify a historical topic and do the analysis to answer the question about that particular aspect. Whereas in Students as Researchers, they were exploring the whole notion of schooling: *Why be there and what are the things that go wrong with it? Why is it working, why isn't it working?* Instead of a very general question, they actually focused in on themselves, to articulate critically their own selves as learners.

Beyond the classroom, school leaders also spoke of the value of taking an inquiry approach to the kinds of questions or problems that arose in their own practice. Tom, an elementary school principal, spoke in these terms:

> It's applicable to so many things, whether it's a problem that occurs, or when you're working with kids' behavior management, it's about decatastrophizing. It offers a framework to break things down. You just keep asking why, so you actually keep going deeper and deeper until you actually get to: This is what I really want to know.

Integrating an inquiry approach into his leadership meant that Tom could shift from reactive crisis management to analysis. First, this meant that rather than immediately naming a problem ("This child is behaving badly"), the focus turned to questioning the situation ("Why is this child behaving in this way?"). Second, adopting an inquiry framework meant that the situation could be considered in terms of all the possible elements that could be contributing to the problem. Each of these could also be subject to questioning. Although this process took longer than an immediate reaction, it was efficient in the long term because it prevented problems from spiraling.

INNOVATIONS IMPACTING ON THE STUDENTS OF MOST CONCERN

Inquiry encouraged teachers to attempt practices that were significantly different from their usual pedagogies or that used different resources. However, it was less the features of these innovations that teachers recalled most vividly, and more the responses of particular students. It was as if the challenging, struggling students served as the litmus test of innovations. Recall that a decision to integrate a new strategy into one's arsenal is a serious matter for teachers (Everitt, 2012). One of the criticisms teachers often have is of being trapped in a cycle of innovation and reform for its own sake

(Brand, 2009; Hustler, McNamara, Jarvis, Londra, & Campbell, 2003). When a new approach proved able to help the lowest-achieving or most disengaged students, it was worth all the effort. It seems that for our informants, practitioner research was at its most powerful when it served their ethical commitments to struggling students.

Alessandra, a high school language teacher, reported that her most impactful project had introduced her to a new way of thinking about language structure. Rather than the grammatical functions of individual words, she focused on larger units of meaning. What convinced her of the value of this approach was the change it made for her lowest-achieving students:

> You're not looking at adjectives and you're not looking at adverbs, but you're looking at nominal groups and the adjectives with a noun group, so you're seeing blocks of language. And that's quite powerful, especially for students who don't have good literacy skills.

Alessandra was committed to improving. She described herself as someone who "goes home every night and reflects on how you can do that better." Seeing the difference in the students of most concern motivated Alessandra to maintain this new approach within her repertoire of practices for teaching language.

Although practitioner inquiry is not the only means by which educators encounter and try out innovative practices, when teachers took the time to gather and analyze data, they were able to more fully understand how their innovations were working in practice. Importantly, they gained some fine-grained perspectives not only on whether the strategy worked but also for whom. Some teachers spoke of witnessing turning points in the learning careers of individuals for whom regular teaching strategies had not succeeded in the past.

Mimi had taken up and researched a play-based approach to math in her junior primary class. This was very different from her usual method, which combined teacher mini-lectures with small-group mathematics tasks and individual worksheets. Using the play approach, children were oriented to scenarios where role-playing of mathematical practices was integrated, such as shopping or being an explorer. Mimi's data enabled her to compare student outcomes from the play-based approach compared with those from her usual methods. Most striking was the difference for those students whose math achievement had been the most worrying.

This inquiry did not just benefit students in that one class but transformed Mimi's entire orientation to teaching math:

> Math has been a real focus for me. I mean it always has been [a focus] but since I did the practitioner inquiry . . . [t]eaching math is

now a real passion of mine, especially when you have those children that really struggle, and I love being able to find a way to help them understand.

Experiencing success with engaging these struggling students, and having the evidence to demonstrate this to herself, was a significant game changer for Mimi. From being a duty, teaching math became a passion and the play-based approach became a key tool in her repertoire.

Joan's inquiry was in the field of robotics. She had taken up an opportunity to collaborate with a specialist educational technology service, The School of the Future. In visits to the facility and follow-up work in class, her upper elementary students learned principles and applications of robotics. Joan's inquiry project documented and analyzed student responses and learning outcomes.

For Joan, the litmus test of inquiry was Dan, a student with a diagnosed learning disability, who was doing very poorly in written tasks, which was reflected in low grades across the curriculum. Joan knew that Dan had potential but she had not yet found the way to unlock it:

I mean, his reading and writing was hopeless, fair enough, but you could see something was there. . . . I'd nag [all the students] to record in their notebooks, little bits and pieces as they went along. I'd nag and nag and nag and he just didn't.

The change for Dan began with a change in Joan's own understanding of learning practices in science. The robotics specialist encouraged students to plan and document using visual and symbolic notations. This challenged Joan to expand her understanding of how students communicate their learning. She had previously always required written reports for assessment and, knowing that some of her students were resistant to writing, had attempted to scaffold their work through the use of notebooks and encouragement to write "little bits and pieces."

When Joan came to the realization that there were alternative ways of communicating knowledge, she changed the kinds of demands she made on Dan. She recalled a critical moment in a science class, after the robotics project had finished. As usual, Dan was not being very productive:

I said, "I want to see what you've recorded today, and that's the end of it." And he sat there and was grumpy and horrible, and he said, "I can't write it." I said, "I didn't say you had to *write* it; I said you had to *record* it." And it was like a light bulb moment, and he drew these incredibly detailed little pictures of what his project was looking like, and with little arrows and, you know, little basic notes. . . . And for him the turnaround was just incredible.

Later, when Dan was in high school studying math and science, he and Joan talked about this moment. Dan told her he remembers thinking, "What's in my head can actually come down on paper and it is actually valuable, what I'm thinking."

The change in Joan's practice persisted in the long term; she continued to recognize visual documentation as a legitimate means of recording and communicating knowledge in science. This did not benefit Dan alone, yet it was the change in Dan that so powerfully convinced Joan of the educational rationale for the change.

THE VALUE OF THE STUDENT CASE

When teachers' work is judged by the average rise in test scores for a class or school, the individual student experience is considered to be of little account. However, as we have argued above, this averaging mentality did not reflect how these teachers judged their own effectiveness. Rather, potential new strategies were assessed for their value in making a difference to a small group of struggling individuals. A significant turnaround for one student could be the most important test and could strongly reinforce the rationale for continuing with a practice.

For some of the educators, a lasting impact of their adoption of an inquiring orientation was that the individual case was seen as capable of informing practice in a meaningful way. As an elementary school principal, Tom was responsible for developing school improvement plans that were mandated by the state government. School plans were framed in terms of schoolwide improvement goals, such as lifting literacy scores on standardized tests. Drawing on his experience as a practitioner inquirer, Tom changed the focus:

> We're looking at test results and how we can improve those because that's what you do as a school. But I have been asking teachers specifically to think about one child. Rather than it be, you know, "Let's improve . . .", instead it's about asking: "What can you do for this child? What are the things you would specifically do and how will you know it's happened?"

By asking each of his staff to look at a single child, Tom engaged them more meaningfully in the process of analyzing the evidence. He also facilitated an inquiry approach to educational intervention by asking teachers what evidence could be gathered to inform them about the success of their efforts. It is this sense of accountability to students that markedly characterized these teacher researchers and was reinforced through the practice of inquiry.

IMPACTS ON ROLES OTHER THAN CLASSROOM TEACHING

Not all the educators in the IPI cohort were classroom teachers or school leaders. Some operated in specialist roles such as learning support or counseling. Although these educators were a minority in the cohort, their accounts of practice impacts are worthy of notice. School counselors have a practice that often involves responding to student problems both inside and outside school contexts. Their clientele often includes the students classroom teachers would identify as those of most concern.

For these practitioners, the two main kinds of impact were similar to those of the classroom-based educators, but experienced in a different professional role. First, they integrated an inquiry orientation into their practice and, second, their innovations succeeded in making a difference for some of the most challenging students.

Matthew worked in a high school in a large rural town where early school dropout was a significant problem. As the school counselor, he was aware of a group of students who were "off the books," describing them as the "hidden young people." Living in the town, Matthew knew many of these school leavers were suffering from poor mental and physical health, at risk of substance abuse, and lacking family support. Some could no longer live at home and so were "couch surfing" at friends' places.

Matthew determined to build an inquiry around these young people with the aim of mobilizing service providers to respond more effectively. He initially surveyed youth to discover their circumstances and reasons for leaving school. There were some surprises and challenges to Matthew's beliefs about what disengaged students wanted and needed. He had been convinced of the value of vocational education for students who were not succeeding in academic courses. However, the survey showed that some of the students who left school did so because they had not wanted to be slotted into the vocational strand and found these courses limited and uninspiring. Matthew realized that his low expectations had contributed to limiting options for these students:

> I thought that if we just add to their curriculum a lot of vocational stuff, that will be good to get them on their way . . . but some kids were really academically brilliant, and other kids who weren't wanted more than that. And a lot of the vocational courses are at that really low level: Step 1: *This is how you wash your hands.* . . . That higher-order, critical thinking seems to be lacking.

Two outcomes came from this. First, Matthew addressed the youths' practical and well-being issues by initiating meetings with service providers. Rather than solving the problem, these discussions generated more perspectives, which Matthew incorporated into his analysis:

All the services that are meant to be there and active and supporting young people can't do it, because what we learned was they're catering to those kids or those parents who are able to make appointments and keep them, who are able to read the [information]. They know how to do it, yeah, but these kids didn't.

This ultimately led to a set of strategies that improved services' ability to cater to these youth. The local mental health service increased its staffing, the school developed flexible arrangements for attendance, and one by one young people began returning to school. However, school itself also needed to change. The second outcome was introducing the creative, critical thinking element that had been missing in the vocationally oriented curriculum. Matthew worked with a group of educators to develop curriculum that oriented the youth as resources for their communities, utilizing their life experiences to inquire, creatively express, and communicate authentic issues:

So we came up with this magazine that represented these kids' views of life and what the issues were, and it meant that you were ticking all the boxes for your SACE [high school diploma]. . . . It was like a Pied Piper program. If it resonated with kids, then they'd do it; if it didn't they wouldn't. So we were kind of there on our merits only and if we worked successfully then the kids would come. So that happened.

The overall outcome of this complex process of exploration, inquiry, and response was a dual reengagement. Not only were the youth reengaged with education but, probably more important, the school and services reengaged with the youth. The educators saw themselves as being put to the test: "there on our merits only." The turnaround was not just in students returning to school but in the shift in their status. They had been considered, in Matthew's words, "antisocial kids who don't want to learn," and by dropping out they had become invisible and forgotten. They became visible again, invested with potential and resources for their communities, and, against the odds, they became school graduates.

CONCLUSION

Educators are constantly under pressure to improve their practice in order to improve student learning outcomes. In recent decades, there have been successive waves of reforms, aimed at getting teachers to change what they are doing in the classroom. The logic of these reforms is the same for the problem as it is for the solution. The problem is the poor performance of students on mandated standardized assessments, and the success of reforms is likewise judged on the extent to which test scores increase

(Welner & Mathis, 2015). Scientific research that meets the "gold standard" of large-scale experimental studies, in which a control group is compared to an intervention group, has been translated into curriculum delivery packages comprising resources such as textbooks, professional development programs, and assessment instruments (Cunningham, 2001). Investigations have sought to determine whether, and to what extent, teachers are implementing mandated programs and approaches with fidelity—that is, exactly as specified.

We are currently in a period where a compromise is being suggested in some quarters, which maintains the compulsory nature of scientifically based programs but seeks to harness teachers' ability to adapt approaches to their students. This compromise position allows schools and teachers to modify "evidence-based" programs and strategies to make them more effective for local conditions (Guttierez & Penuel, 2014). It is suggested that these local adaptations, if proven successful, could be accumulated into a bank of approved variations. This controlled adaptation process, termed *improvement science*, takes up aspects of action research but without explicitly acknowledging its history as an established approach to teacher inquiry (Lewis, 2015). By a circuitous route, reformers seem to have arrived at a kind of practitioner inquiry, albeit a reduced version that consists of quick trials or "rapid testing of promising ideas" (Lewis, 2015, p. 55). Regardless of whether programs are imposed wholesale or subjected to allowed degrees of adaptation, the success or failure of these initiatives continues to be primarily judged by student achievement on standardized tests.

The experiences of the inquiring educators whose stories are recounted in this chapter depart from both these models; they neither followed a script nor adapted a mandated program to produce a system-approved local variation. In neither of these approaches would teachers get to design an intervention based on their own professional judgment about the learning needs of their students. This is not to suggest that adaptation of mandated programs cannot be a route to improvement—it can—but it would struggle to be a dynamic, flexible, creative, and passionate inquiring orientation. Over time, many of these teachers integrated an inquiring orientation into their practice so that questioning became habitual; when a question was asked, the next step was to generate evidence.

The relationship between the practices of inquiry and the practices of education can be thought of in terms of praxis (Groundwater-Smith, Mitchell, & Mockler, 2016). Praxis is the enactment of the "moral agency" of the educator who is concerned with ensuring that rights to learning and growth are realized (Latta & Kim, 2010, p. 137). A desire to serve students has been identified as one of the most powerful incentives for improvement, as it connects with "intrinsic motivators that bring teachers into teaching in the first place" (O'Day, 2002, p. 317). These educators came to inquiry already committed to improving the learning experiences and outcomes of the lowest-achieving and most disengaged students. Low test scores were part of the picture, but equally as significant to the teachers were factors such as low morale, rejection of mainstream schooling, boredom, and also hints of a glowing ember of intelligence and purpose. These sparks motivated teachers to keep trying to find keys to unlocking student potential.

These educators were the kind of people who went home every night and thought about what they could do better, who actively feared turning into the "crusty teacher who teaches from a textbook." Practitioner inquiry provided them with support for innovation, a framework for analyzing their practice, and a means of determining what could make a difference for their students. That the crucial test of success was whether these innovations made a difference to the students of most concern demonstrates their commitment to praxis.

CHAPTER 3

Impacts in the School

"It just builds that culture of learning and sharing"

This chapter will discuss the ways in which educators' participation in practitioner inquiry had impacts beyond their own learning and their own students' outcomes. Whether through the exercise of formal leadership or collegial influence, as a planned program of change, or through opportunistic teachable moments with peers, the ripple effect was felt in their schools. We will argue that the effectiveness of these teachers as change agents was shaped by their experience of practitioner inquiry. We will suggest that this was, to some extent, a function of the ways in which inquiry communities built skills for participation in complex adaptive systems.

Over the past decade, we have seen a shift in ways of understanding schools and other institutions away from hierarchical models to complex systems or networks (Snyder, 2013). A reliance on top-down power structures of imposed school accountability has been identified as a limiting factor in achieving improvements in student learning outcomes (O'Day, 2002). The pace of societal and technological change has also driven an argument for reconceptualizing education and schools in terms of complex adaptive systems (Snyder, 2013). In this new view, "we understand schools not as bureaucracies or as hierarchies but as communities or ecologies" (Poeter, Badiali, & Hammond, 2000, p. 162). Educational change, from this perspective, requires negotiation of "organizational structures, norms, practices, and patterns of social relationships [and] how these organizational features are connected to the broader social and cultural environment" (Anagnostopoulos, Sykes, McCrory, Cannata, & Frank, 2010, p. 340).

Educational reform by its nature requires change at every level and throughout schools (Fullan, 2006). However, top-down, compliance-oriented accountability systems have had limited effects on schools' organizational cultures (Reilly, 2009). Unless teachers' hearts and minds are engaged, it is all too possible to pay lip service to, or actively subvert, reform efforts. This can apply even when a reform involves implementing practitioner inquiry at a whole-school level. Indeed, evidence points to the difficulty of enlisting entire staffs into the practice of inquiry. Looking for schools in which this had been achieved, Berger and colleagues found them to be few and far between (Berger, Boles & Troen, 2005). The three cases they eventually settled on included only one school in which every member of the teaching staff and the leadership were active researchers as part of their normal professional practice. In another school, the principal attempted to mandate inquiry for all teachers but faced a revolt, forcing it to become a choice taken up by just half of the faculty. The third case had a small subgroup of active teacher researchers whose work was known only to members of that group.

Perhaps the problem lies in thinking of a school as a single entity into which a change will come in a singular way. Network and ecological models are changing how we think of schools and thus of the process of change (Fullan, 2004, 2006; Poeter, Badialia, & Hammond, 2000). Reporting for the Organisation for Economic Co-operation and Development (OECD), Snyder (2013) summarizes this view as "a new lens that focuses on the complex interactions of the actors within educational systems and subsystems, creating a broader view of educational systems as a holistic organism" (p. 6).

School accountability drives have not always paid sufficient attention to this. O'Day (2002) conducted a close examination of school-based accountability in a Chicago school district. She argues that one of the dilemmas of such movements is that "The school is the unit of intervention, yet the individual is the unit of action" (p. 295). In a bureaucratic hierarchical model of systemic change, an individual is not considered a significant unit. Indeed, as O'Day (2002) notes, the Chicago reforms "offer[ed] few incentives for individuals to improve their practice" (p. 312). From a complexity perspective, however, individual actors and particular events can have significant effects on the larger system. That is because, according to this theory, systems emerge as a result of interactions between individual agents and adapt in response to feedback passing continuously among members of the system (Snyder, 2013).

Looking at the actions of individuals or specific events or practices can provide a way to understand how complex systems, such as educational systems, are behaving. In this approach, the analyst will "focus in on the specific node of interest and then explore its sphere of influence rather than only the node itself or the entirety of the ecosystem" (Snyder, 2013, p. 15). Anagnostopoulos and colleagues (2010) did this when they focused on the impacts of National Board–certified teachers in their schools. These teachers were seen as examples of "carriers," actors who "transport new organizational forms across and within organizational fields and sectors [and] shape whether new forms take hold" (Anagnostopoulos et al., 2010, p. 340). Thus, it is necessary to conceive of schools in terms of interactions among individuals while at the same time attempting to shape the context so that these interactions are productive for the goal of education. Fullan (2004) puts it this way:

[I]f you want to change systems, you need to increase the amount of purposeful interaction between and among *individuals* . . . and indeed within and across *systems*. (p. 4)

In this chapter, we will consider the IPI teachers as actors whose strategic and sometimes spontaneous intervention mobilized action in their schools. First, we will review the evidence from our IPI survey regarding the impacts that participants identified at the school level. Then, we will discuss themes from the interviews that express ways in which educators were able to influence colleagues, drawing on skills or knowledge that they had built as inquirers.

THE IPI SURVEY

The IPI survey asked informants about the ways in which they informed colleagues about their inquiries and about evidence that their inquiring activities impacted on professional practice at their sites. Most of the practitioners communicated about their inquiries with colleagues through a presentation (84%) as well as in less formal ways. Just under half (45%) ran one or more professional development sessions related to the subject of their inquiry. A third (33%) wrote a research report specifically for their principal or manager.

Three kinds of school-level impacts were investigated through the survey: on practice, on resources, and on the nature of collegial conversations. A similar number of informants—about half the cohort—reported these kinds of impacts. New practices were adopted (53%) and resources generated from inquiries were taken up by others (53%). A change in the nature of teacher conversations was reported by 47% of informants. Impacts on school-level policies were not as common. Just 21% of informants reported this kind of impact.

For a minority of the group (22%), no changes flowed beyond their own practice. A similar amount (16%) had not presented findings to school colleagues and thus their inquiries were conducted purely for their own learning. This suggests that reporting to colleagues is an important element in making new knowledge, practice, and resources available to colleagues. Clearly, this does not always produce a flow-on effect. A smaller percentage reported impacts on colleagues' practices than communicated about their inquiries to colleagues. However, as the interviewees show, communication practices were vital in opening up a space for change to circulate through the school ecology.

To help us understand how practitioners, many of whom were not formal leaders, could function as change agents, we will now consider some themes that arose from analysis of the interviews. First, we will consider the importance of opportunistic, teachable moments with colleagues. Then, we will look at the strategy of working small to seed larger change. Finally, we will consider, as a connecting theme, the role of discourse in the mobilization of new ways of talking, thinking, and acting through professional communities.

"GOOD LEARNING JUST IN PASSING": THE TEACHABLE MOMENT

We have suggested that in a complex system, the role of an individual may potentially be more significant than would be apparent in a hierarchical model. Teachers are familiar with the concept of the teachable moment in a classroom context (Thompson, 2008). Orienting to the possibility of teachable moments requires educators to be responsive to moment-by-moment interactions in the classroom. Experienced educators are on the lookout for subtle cues that a student or a group of students is receptive to a timely intervention, perhaps because an impasse has been reached in attempting to reach a learning goal.

This concept can be extended to interactions with colleagues. Reilly (2009) has argued that professional learning often occurs "in the flow of dynamic encounters" (p. 94). She suggests that those wanting to understand this process should "attend to the comings and goings of people" and to places where activity "appears most lively" (p. 94). Life in schools has a lot of "coming and going" to it. Teachers, when not in their classrooms, can be found traveling the corridors, passing rooms, lining up for coffee, browsing a bulletin board, or stopping to have a quick chat. The coming and going can also be understood in relation to the flux of change with policy, curriculum, and technological initiatives continually making new demands on teachers.

The interviews with the IPI teachers helped us understand how change might occur in the "flow of dynamic encounters." Let us look at a case in point. Here, Ben, an English teacher in an all-boy K–12 school in a working-class neighborhood, describes an interaction with colleagues that occurred without planning:

> I was passing the staff room the other day and the ESL [English as a second language] teacher was writing a grant trying to get some money for something. . . . [T]he English coordinator was there, and he often comes to me and asks me (it's interesting, because he's the faculty coordinator but I'm the literacy, key literacy teacher, so it's similar but different, we complement each other, I guess) but as I was walking past they asked me to have my input . . . and I said, "Well . . .", and I gave them some ideas.
>
> They wanted these particular books but they didn't understand how to spend the money. . . . I said, "If you go and apply for the

books, you're not going to get the money, because it's just a resource. They need to see active engagement, teachers becoming more like learners, and understanding and developing pedagogy rather than just applying to get funds to get some books."

About a year earlier, Ben had completed an inquiry aimed at engaging boys in literacy, as part of a cluster of schools in the Catholic system (see Chapter 6). One of the flow-on effects of the project for him personally was winning a grant to undertake some further classroom research. From his account above, it is clear that he had gained the confidence of his subject-area senior, who was in the habit of consulting Ben on literacy-related matters. His narrative makes it clear that he was responding to an invitation, rather than imposing his expertise on peers in an unsolicited manner.

Based on his understanding of the genre and discourse of funding applications, Ben immediately identified a key problem. He could see that, like many novice grant seekers, his colleagues had focused on product rather than process. That is, they had first determined an object on which to spend the money rather than a rationale for how they would use it and why it was needed. He could see that the application needed to use the discourse of the funding provider in order to make its case. To assist his peers, Ben introduced terms from this discourse: *active engagement* and *developing pedagogy*.

The books that Ben's colleagues wanted to purchase were grammar books for ESL students. These students were integrated into classes with peers whose English was much more established, and teachers felt frustrated working with such divergent language abilities. Ben could hear in his colleagues' talk their hope that the books would be a fix. He did not try to dissuade them from spending money on grammar books. He listened to their priorities and then attempted to make a connection with educational principles:

> I was able to discuss ways that they could use the books: "To use the books for this, you'll need time to develop pedagogies to engage the students in their learning," and so, and I said, "That's fine, use that, but also use different types of literacies and make it your application that you're going to focus on teacher development and professional development around multiliteracies." . . . Yeah, it was good because there was the English coordinator, the ESL teacher, and a couple of the English teachers, and they were taking in and drawing on it.

Ben described this incident as "good learning just in passing." This kind of learning plays to teachers' professional dispositions to span their environment and take advantage of teachable moments. By taking up this opportunity, Ben was able to have a significant impact on a group of colleagues, some of whom had formal leadership positions. His skillful reading of professional social relations meant that he was able to function as an expert without disrupting the school's organizational hierarchy.

CATALYZING CHANGE THROUGH SMALL BEGINNINGS

Educational research is often challenged to "scale up" to achieve widespread reform (Anderson & Herr, 2011). The ideal is for a single intervention to be teacher-proofed so that it can be rolled out across entire school systems. Such programs require top-down design, resourcing, and regulation (Reilly, 2009). However, as we have discussed, complexity models of schooling open up the possibility that small interventions might have much larger effects. Some accounts of the IPI teachers gave evidence that small-scale projects and individual actions could set off a ripple effect through schools and beyond.

Penny was in her second year of working in a school that provides services to students who are unable to attend regular school because of geographical isolation, chronic illness, and school refusal. This school had been developing its web-based delivery. Although excited about these changes, Penny observed that the learning model was still too reliant on teacher transmission. There was a low level of interaction online, with most students accessing information and submitting assignments rather than sharing or discussing their learning. She takes up the story:

> My job is to get other people to get into e-learning and to develop their practice, and to make it more student-centered. Now if I can use inquiry and get a core of teachers involved in that, then that's much more powerful than me trotting off and doing it by myself. Gilly Salmon is a lecturer, a university lecturer in London, and she was one of the very first to use online discussion, and she came up with a system for facilitating online discussion. She was here in Australia and I went along to one of her sessions. So, I was able to bring that back and incorporate that [into my teaching]. I guess that was my first little mini, on my own, project that got me going.
>
> And I was able to use that to encourage staff. Everyone who tried it got the Gilly Salmon notes and away they went, and out of that we built up our own [strategies]. And different faculties with their different approaches, you know, science built up their own set of strategies. So we sort of hived off from there, and then what they did became part of the next level of action research. The science people here were heavily involved with me right from the start so they've done some great stuff, and as a result they're one of the most innovative faculties here, so I think that's an indication of its worth. I

mean, I think the fact that the school wants to try and get this going across the whole school is an indication of how well these small pockets have worked.

I think they turned it into something bigger, and other schools went for it, now that I remember. Yeah, that's what they did but I've lost interest, because I only like the small projects, targeted projects, where I can work with small groups of teachers.

As Penny began researching strategies to improve online engagement, she discovered the work of Professor Gilly Salmon and what she heard made her want to implement Salmon's (2002) approach to facilitating on-line discussion for learning. Penny's choice to run her first inquiry as a "little mini, on my own, project" was deliberate. She had led larger-scale collaborative projects in her previous school. However, Penny was new to this school and to teaching at a distance. Her base of influence was not yet established. And she was trying Salmon's strategies for the first time. Once she was satisfied that the approach was producing results in terms of increased interactivity and more student online engagement, she was ready to take her learning to the staff.

Penny was not interested in leading or steering a whole-school reform as much as in catalyzing activity. As she reported, further developments happened in the context of faculty groups. Though she maintained a connection with her own science faculty, she was not aware in detail of what was happening elsewhere. Indeed, Penny heard that the movement had later grown beyond the school. Penny identified herself as a small-group specialist and inquiry as her key strategy. Through her actions, she catalyzed activity and was content to see her colleagues developing their professional knowledge and practice.

At the same time, by connecting with an international scholar, Penny was introducing her colleagues to developments that linked them with a wider context. In this case, it might be said that Salmon was engaged in a scaling-up process, by circulating her ideas through education systems globally using traditional professional development strategies. In this multi-layered networking of innovation, experimentation, and inquiry, individual practitioners like Penny are key players.

CHANGING THE DISCOURSE

It is through communication that professional knowledge and experience can be shared in education workplaces. However, for communication to be part of change, there needs to be change in the nature of the communication, either in its content or process, or both. Communicational business as usual in school staff rooms is shaped by social norms of egalitarianism

(Anagnostopoulos et al., 2010). This leveling culture constrains teachers in various ways. They may be "reluctant to share professional successes" for fear of seeming to put themselves above colleagues (Schechter, 2012, p. 69). They may "avoid fault-lines" by limiting themselves to "generalities about instructional practice" (Selkriga & Keamya, 2014, p. 426).

Even when educators join a professional learning community (PLC), in which talking about issues of practice is the core business, these norms can be hard to shift. One professional learning project, for instance, found that in PLCs focused on improving mathematics pedagogy, teachers "talk[ed] past each other with little discussion of student learning" (Clark, Moore, &Carlson, 2008, p. 298). The research team decided to deliberately and explicitly change the nature of the conversation by introducing and modeling the practice of "speaking with meaning." Facilitators were trained in this purposeful and conceptually informed style of communication and were directed to introduce it to their PLCs. Over time, the conversation in the PLCs changed: "teachers began to hold each other accountable for providing more meaningful explanations" (Clark, Moore, & Carlson, 2008, p. 303).

Some professional learning researchers use the ideas of language theorist Bakhtin to explore how the professional language of educators is implicated in their learning. Reilly (2009) notes that professional learning "often requires teachers to learn another's discourse" (p. 220). However, this requirement is often imposed in a context of hierarchical relationships—in other words as a top-down, one-way move. Bakhtin (1981) makes a distinction between authoritative and dialogic discourse. Official policy and system mandates come with their own language—authoritative discourse— that teachers are expected to adopt. Authoritative discourse can be seen as alien: "it exists in other people's mouths, in other people's contexts, serving other people's intentions" (Bakhtin, 1981, p. 294). This can give grounds for resistance. However, through dialogue in which these alien terms are brought into contact with one's familiar discourse, there is a chance to test their applicability. As we saw with Clark and colleagues' (2008) mathematics PLCs, the teachers eventually found that the concept of "speaking with meaning" enabled them to accomplish valued professional goals, and so they found a place in their language for this concept.

The IPI teachers' accounts helped us understand more about how this process can happen in action. We saw how changing the discourse can facilitate the ripple effect as language acts to bring new ideas into dialogue with familiar ways of speaking and thinking.

Rosemary: "Language that we have been able to use"

Rosemary was part of an inquiry project focused on the literacy demands of the senior secondary curriculum in which the authors were academic research partners. The teacher research partners were introduced to a framework for analyzing curriculum that they applied to tracking the literacy demands they made of students. Rosemary recalled the experience of encountering the new language of this framework:

> You talked about "meta this" and "meta that," and I remember the eyes going around the table going, "What are they talking about?" But by the time you'd finished we knew, and we could use it ourselves. So it wasn't perhaps language that we had used; it is maybe language that we have been able to use since in work that we have done with our colleagues.

Recalling herself at the beginning of the process, Rosemary expresses her unfamiliarity with the language. Initially, she couldn't even use the new terms; they were just word-objects ("meta this" and "meta that"). This alien language was not even answerable with language; the teacher participants reacted nonverbally, the "eyes going around the table" signaling to one another their noncomprehension.

As Rosemary and the other teachers became more familiar with the conceptual language, it became knowledge rather than just words ("we knew, and we could use it ourselves"). This reflects a shift in the nature of the inquiry group to becoming a discourse community—that is, one with a shared language. From the authoritative language being owned by the academic partners, it became a genuine tool for the teachers. We hear this shift when Rosemary changes her pronouns from second person ("you talked") to the collective "we knew." In taking up new language and making it their own, Rosemary and her peers had something with which to "work . . . with our colleagues." Thus, the conclusion of the initial inquiry was the beginning of a new round of dialogue in Rosemary's workplace, where she became a key promoter of inquiry.

Siobhan: "I'm sounding like you now"

Siobhan was another IPI member who described this phenomenon. A primary school principal, Siobhan was a member of the Inclusive Education inquiry project (see Chapter 5). Her school was in an area of high economic disadvantage and her staff was always stretched trying to deliver a high-quality education to students whose lives outside of school were affected by poverty and disruption.

As she began to engage in conversations with the project group and read in the area of inclusion, Siobhan found herself rethinking aspects of her school's work with challenging and disadvantaged students. Her immediate impulse was to bring this thinking to her staff:

I've had these aha moments, and I have to share it with everybody because this is the new world, because that was old world, and now this is the new world, and this is the thinking.

In sharing her aha moments, Siobhan modeled to her team what it is to open oneself up to new ways of thinking about education. She realized this was risky because her staff already faced so many demands in their daily work:

There are times when you know that they think, "Oh, she's as nutty as a fruitcake now. She's off on another tangent." . . . You can see them go, "Oh no!," and I say, "It's all right, it's all right, it's going to be better."

Siobhan acknowledges here that teachers apply a strict test to demands on their time and thinking—the test of relevance to practice. With a continual stream of initiatives coming from the Department of Education, many of them directed at schools whose students were not doing well in standardized tests, teachers faced reform fatigue. These demands were often experienced as a diversion from their core business—"another tangent."

However, Siobhan was convinced that "there's so much more that can be done and needs to be done" to achieve genuine inclusion for students with disabilities, learning difficulties, and serious life challenges. In particular, she wanted to bring a strength-based, success-oriented approach to her staff's work with the most challenging students. She asked them to monitor how they talked about and with these students, to always find a concrete achievable goal for the next step of learning, and to make their feedback consistently constructive. These students had often experienced years of academic failure, had rarely heard praise, were often angry, and were quick to relegate themselves to the scrap heap.

Siobhan wanted staff to become aware of and to challenge their own negative mindsets and to challenge students to do the same. Years later, she can still see and hear the ripple effect. She gives an example of overhearing the specialist teacher working with children on the autism spectrum saying to one child, "It's not really as bad as you think it is, so let's get some change to that thinking; how can we think differently now?" She found that conflicts and flashpoints in classes were more often being reframed. Siobhan gives a case:

There was a kid, she was in real trouble at the beginning of the year, and now she's in less trouble and she's going to get there and she'll graduate through grade 7 without it being as big a drama as it was going to be.

Teachers at this school are aware of a change in their language and of Siobhan's influence in bringing about this change. Referring again to the specialist teacher, Siobhan reported:

> She said, "I'm sounding like you now, Siobhan," and I said, "Well, that's a really good thing." She said, "I know it is, this is working, but it comes out of my mouth." . . . She was sharing with another teacher, the teacher said, "I can hear your voice coming through here."

This speaks to the power of language as a carrier of professional knowledge. We also see how language's ability to become internalized and emerge as speech can be experienced as somewhat discomfiting. There is a sense that the new way of talking is coming from outside the person, even when it is clearly being spoken by him or her. As teachers in Siobhan's school began to focus on their language, they began to hear what they "sound[ed] like." Their talk became the object of talk. This is somewhat counter to the usual rules of conversation in which participants are meant to focus on the content rather than comment on *how* a person talks.

According to Bakhtin, this conscious work with language is part of the shift from authoritative (top-down) to dialogic communication. Writing under the name Voloshinov (1986), he explains:

> To understand another person's utterance means to orient yourself with respect to it, to find a proper place for it in the corresponding context. . . . *Any true understanding is dialogic in nature.* (p. 102)

Siobhan's teachers were engaged in "find[ing] a proper place" for the positive, strength-based language that she had introduced. In this process, what had been taken for granted in their speech was brought to their attention. Without these changes in talk, Siobhan is convinced that her school would not have moved in the direction of greater inclusion.

Dealing with the Curly Questions

For professional conversations to become dialogic, there must be genuine openness to engaging with different viewpoints. However, staff room debates often run like well-rehearsed scripts. Those with an ax to grind air their familiar preoccupations while colleagues wait for the scene to run its course. From the accounts of some of the IPI teachers, their experience with practitioner inquiry changed the way they engaged with these conversations. Questions from colleagues were treated as invitations to explain and demonstrate their knowledge. Feeling confident about being able to address these challenges respectfully enabled these encounters.

Denise worked in a small rural school that had been experiencing challenges related to students' performance on standardized tests. She commented that "the tone and quality of our learning conversations actually seemed to decrease the more stress we had." The principal was supportive of Denise, along with a colleague, enrolling in an inquiry-focused postgraduate study program focused on science teaching.

Through her participation in the inquiry project, Denise gained experience in sharing her ideas with peers. It was a big change from the "admin, admin, admin, nitty-gritty" staff room conversations she was used to. Through her reading and involvement in discussions, she began to "get those really deep theoretical ideas" and make connections to her practice.

When Denise and her colleague brought their learning back to their school community, they faced some challenging questions. The inquiry approach to science learning, which was the focus of Denise's inquiry, was seen by some colleagues as inappropriate, particularly for younger students:

> A couple of the middle primary [teachers] were, I suppose, kind of anti to start off with because [they said] *kids can't possibly question; they can't pose investigable questions.*

Prior to joining the inquiry community, Denise had been reluctant to take on this kind of challenge. Consistent with Schechter's (2012) findings, she did not want to be seen as putting herself above her colleagues, or, as she put it, "blowing your own trumpet." However, with the support of her peer and with a firm grasp on her own knowledge and evidence, Denise was able to engage in a robust dialogue with her colleagues:

> When the curly questions come from teachers and you're actually showing them what you've done—this is the practice and this is the change—and they go, "Why, why should this change?" then you can say, "Well, the way kids learn is . . . and if you put that into practice then constructivism comes into it like this, and therefore this is what we need to be doing."

Rob also found that his experience of practitioner inquiry gave him "a basis to talk from." An elementary school principal, he had gathered a group of staff to collaborate on an inquiry process. It concerned a problem troubling to many teachers: students missing class because of poor attendance and behavioral suspension. He describes the conversations that occurred as the team worked through their survey and interview data:

> "We've found this information, we've found this out, it's been really valuable, what are the practical things that we can do?" But then all the other questions that came out from it. "How is it that we actually

rejig our timetable to actually get this to work better for all kids? What are the things we can do to help parents actually be informed about what's happening?"

Because the inquiry process generated questions as well as findings, it opened up space for constructive professional dialogue in the school.

Colleen had been investigating ways to increase students' information literacy, particularly focusing on their ability to evaluate and use online learning resources. Her principal asked her to run a "spotlight session" to share her findings with staff. She focused on the educational aspects of her project:

[Students] really getting conceptual development and understanding, and therefore being able to apply that to their skills and demonstrate their learning.

However, in Colleen's school, staff room debates often wound up being about workload and what some teachers saw as unreasonable demands on their time. Colleen found herself asked to address workload aspects of her teaching:

One of the teachers was really pushing, he asked me a question, and what he was hoping I would say was, "Yes, this has made my work easier," and I had to just say to him, "No, it's not about making my work easier, it's about making it richer, and more effective as part of that."

Colleen took her colleague's question seriously and did not engage in trivial jousting. She shaped the conversation into a dialogue about professional values and kept the lines of communication open. As a result of her willingness to engage with colleagues, regardless of their opinions, Colleen found herself deputized to work with those who were least keen about inquiry:

I had a whole pile of resistant practitioners who didn't want to be involved but knew they had to be involved, so personalizing it to work with them in relation to their curriculum and their development. That was fun, but at times really frustrating.

CONCLUSION: THE SPILLOVER EFFECT

Teachers' participation in practitioner inquiry impacts on more than just their own practice and their own students' learning outcomes. There is a flow-on or spillover effect on colleagues and on their school's professional learning culture. The concept of the spillover effect is taken from Sun and colleagues (2013), who investigated the impacts of a teacher development program, not on the participants themselves but on their colleagues. Based on statistical analysis of longitudinal survey data, the researchers found that "peer effects are close to those of [teachers'] own direct exposure to professional development" (Sun et al., 2013, p. 358). There was a considerable "spillover effect" for teachers who had the opportunity to work alongside those who had participated in the National Writing Project.

The accounts of the IPI teachers help us understand the processes that create these flows of knowledge and practice. First, the survey results indicated a connection between opportunities to communicate inquiry outcomes and changes to colleagues' knowledge and practice. When inquiry is a completely privatized practice, these spillover effects are perhaps unsought and certainly hard to achieve. However, more often educators are alert to "teachable moments" with colleagues and adapt at reading interactional dynamics to understand when the time is right to offer insights, advice, and resources. Practitioner inquiry provided educators with skills to share but also with practice in articulating their knowledge and linking this with evidence. In this sense, the inquiring educators were more willing and able to handle the "curly questions" from peers and to welcome divergent views as resources for problem solving.

The role of language and discourse is central to these ripple effects. New knowledge in collegial communication is most often articulated through speech (or written chat, in the case of online communities). This is a complex process affected by social norms of participation, which in many education workplaces include constraints on what can be said and how. Practitioner inquiry took many of these teachers outside their workplaces and into inquiry communities within which different kinds of language were used. At first, some felt resistance to taking up these alien speech forms; however, they were intrigued by the concepts and so began adopting the language as a means to grasp the conceptual tools. Introducing new ways of talking was integral to accomplishing the kinds of changes they saw as promising. These educators became bearers of discourse into their schools.

CHAPTER 4

Impacts on Career Networks

"Going from strength to strength"

The in-depth retrospective career histories that the IPI educators shared with us has enabled us to recognize ways in which participation in practitioner inquiry has produced career benefits. Teachers at different career stages have experienced these benefits in different ways, from being reenergized as a late-career teacher, to consolidating professional skills in early to mid-career. In this chapter, we argue that a networking perspective holds promise for understanding the nature of career impacts related to practitioner inquiry. We first present relevant findings from the IPI survey. Then we consider career growth in relation to the development of professional networks. The impact of practitioner inquiry on professional networks will be analyzed with reference to three contrasting case studies drawn from network analysis of the IPI teachers' career narratives. Finally, we consider how practitioner inquiry aligns with the new figure of the lead teacher as described in contemporary descriptions of professional standards.

IPI SURVEY FINDINGS: IMPACTS ON PROFESSIONAL PROFILE

In exploring the impact of practitioner inquiry on educators' careers, we used the construct of the "'professional profile." This construct represents how an educator is viewed by peers and is inclusive of activities that bring an educator's professional practice and knowledge to the attention of others in his or her professional community. Note that these professional profile indicators are seen to flow from participation in inquiry—that is, to be a consequence rather than a characteristic of inquiry.

When asked about ways in which they believed their professional profiles had been impacted by their participation in inquiry, around half of the participants (31) believed they were "viewed by colleagues as skilled or knowledgeable." More than half of the group (39) had run professional development for colleagues on a subject related to their inquiry, and 15 of them had written for publication. A significant group (23) had gone on to lead at least one further collaborative inquiry. Being selected for a committee or working group had occurred for 20 of the educators.

Although this experience of enhanced professional profile was not the case for all participants, this is still a significant outcome. When considered in relation to the obstacles to teachers gaining recognition from their peers, it is even more so. In a study of the development of teacher leaders through a school improvement program called Innovative Designs for Enhancing Achievements in Schools (IDEAS) that was carried out across 16 schools, Dawson (2011) identified enablers and challenges. One of the key challenges was teachers' fear of peer policing, aimed at ensuring that individuals were not raised above their peers. This sense of vulnerability to peer judgment was expressed by one of Dawson's (2011) participants:

> Taking on this IDEAS facilitation role was very challenging for me. I got to the stage where I would have done anything for a change but . . . I was not prepared to be "hung out to dry." We have got a group of teachers at our school who crucify anything new and anyone associated with it. (p. 22)

It is not surprising, therefore, that some of the teachers we surveyed identified less positive aspects of the more visible profile created by their participation in inquiry. Eight (8) reported that colleagues had been "dismissive" and five (5) said that peers had been "critical" of their inquiry activities.

Nevertheless, many of the teachers experienced clear positive impacts on their career. Among the group, 18 achieved promotions during the period under question and believed that their participation in inquiry directly contributed to this career goal. When considering how practitioner inquiry might support teachers in their professional careers, we asked about the acquisition of skills that might support career development.

The strongest response was for data analysis, which 42 of the participants (73%) reported as a professional skill developed by their participation in inquiry. The ability to write to a professional or academic level was cited by more than half (34). This is not surprising, as many of them had undertaken inquiry in the context of a program of study. Just over half the cohort (30) had developed new skills in presentation, and 27 had developed new ICT skills. Some of the latter group had undertaken inquiries specifically in the field of ICTs, but others had developed ICT skills while inquiring into other areas.

A third dimension of career impact surveyed was orientation to lifelong learning. Here, we were interested in aspects of learning most related to maintaining an inquiring mindset. We did not ask about general participation in professional development but rather focused on three areas: professional reading, conference attendance, and enrollment in graduate courses. The teachers indicated that their participation in practitioner inquiry had contributed to increased engagement in professional/scholarly reading. Interestingly, although only 50% indicated that they had increased the amount of reading they did, a larger number reported a qualitative shift; that is, they had a greater understanding of the literature they read. A significant group

(24) had attended at least one conference as a result of their inquiry, and about a quarter of the group had gone on to further graduate study.

NETWORKING IN EDUCATORS' CAREER DEVELOPMENT

The role of professional networks in supporting educators' careers has recently been receiving increasing attention (Baker-Doyle, 2011; Engvik, 2014; Mackey & Evans, 2011; Schreurs, 2014). This research has been motivated by finding answers to persistent problems of teacher attrition, isolation, and stagnation. Investigating how educators connect with professional peers and use networks to access valued goods of knowledge, advice, resources, and moral support has yielded some valuable insights. We have drawn on this literature in considering processes by which practitioner inquiry may be involved in the kinds of career progress that the IPI teachers have reported.

In a study of the networking activities of new teachers, Baker-Doyle (2011) identifies two kinds of networks that are professionally significant. *Intentional Professional Networks* are made up of those professional educators that teachers "select to collaborate and interact with to solve professional problems" (Baker-Doyle, 2011, p. 22). These persons are often colleagues at the teachers' school, but not always. The second kind of network is composed of what are termed *Diverse Professional Allies*. This network includes those who, though not professional educators, support the teachers in achieving their professional goals. When educators are transient, these networks may involve colleagues at past schools. These individuals were not called upon to offer specific advice about everyday problems of practice; rather, they were consulted when teachers wanted to discuss professional motives, aspirations, and philosophies.

The importance of individuals in professional networks is emphasized by Snyder (2013) in a discussion of the utility of complexity theory for understanding educational reform (see also Chapter 3). He argues that the quality of individual interactions in a system has consequences beyond those immediately involved. Somewhat clinically, he posits that "targeted applications on the right nodes could create a ripple effect throughout the system" (Snyder, 2013, p. 15). In education systems where there are limited resources, only some teachers can be given certain opportunities such as time out for graduate study. Snyder suggests, however, that when support or resources are directed to an individual practitioner, the benefits potentially extend well beyond that individual. Interactions produce and sustain professional networks, enabling the circulation of resources that include knowledge, support, and demonstrations of practice.

Power relations within schools can have constraining effects on professional networks, particularly when sensitive issues are under discussion. Engvik (2014) found that:

Newly qualified teachers want to establish networks in and outside school that stretch beyond the possibilities power structures provide for professional development. . . . [P]ersonal participant circles that extend into communities and networks outside school are very important. (p. 46)

The issue of power in networks has also been taken up by Coburn (2005) in an investigation of teachers' relationships with what she calls "system actors" and "nonsystem actors" in professional networks. In a context of educational reform, she found that teachers were more likely to change their practice when collaborating with nonsystem actors, such as university academics or professional associations, because they were less regulatory and focused on compliance than were system actors—that is, education departments and school management.

Network analysis has begun to investigate the circulation of professional knowledge and practice within schools. Schreurs (2014) asked teachers to report on their "'learning ties,'" the individuals they would approach, or who approached them, for conversations and collaborations related to professional learning. This analysis showed that although approaching a colleague for advice or support was a general practice for all educators, only a subgroup was regularly approached themselves. This suggests that one possible career path for teachers involves being recognized by colleagues as an expert in a particular subject or professional skill domain. This can occur with or without more formal systems of recognition such as promotion to leadership positions.

In exploring the impact of participation in practitioner inquiry, we wanted to take up the challenge of examining the development of inquiry networks. Our starting assumption was that because participation in inquiry often brings teachers into collaborations beyond their schools, there is potential for the enrichment of professional networks. Using the in-depth interviews as a basis, we applied network analysis using a case study or "ego-centered" approach (Schreurs, 2014) to four educators from different professional contexts, two of whom will be discussed below.

Qualitative network analysis, based on interview data, involves attending to connections among significant events, places, and people in informants' accounts (Noack & Schmidt, 2013; Song & Miskel, 2005). The analysis ordered events into a sequence and employed diagrams representing the development of connections over the period of the career described by informants. In the diagrams, schools are represented by an oval shape and projects by a rectangle, while a six-sided shape is used for university-affiliated nodes, including universities, courses, and individual academics, and the rounded rectangle signifies another organization such as a government department (see Figure 4.1). The changes to a teacher's network over time, with successive inquiry-related experiences, are shown through a series of network diagrams.

Because the teacher interviews were retrospective and often took the form of sequential narratives, we were able to examine changes in networks

Figure 4.1. Key to Shapes Used in Network Diagrams

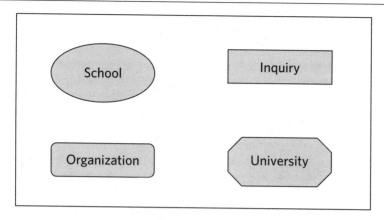

over time. This is shown in the first case below by presenting a succession of network diagrams to demonstrate how connections were made through particular schools, projects, and graduate courses. In subsequent cases, only the full network diagram is provided.

Helen: "This gave me a bedrock"

Helen was a kindergarten teacher in a rural primary/elementary school when she had her first experience of practitioner inquiry. This occurred at a time when the Australian federal government had launched the Quality Teacher Project (QTP) and channeled funds into schools to support professional development with the aim of lifting teacher professionalism. Helen's school had decided to focus its QTP funding on science teaching. After "lots of inservicing," teachers each undertook an action research project focused on science learning in their class. So Helen's initial inquiry network strengthened bonds with her colleagues as well as connecting her with a national teacher improvement program (see Figure 4.2). Helen described sharing her learning with colleagues:

> We did a very quick explanation of what our research showed, and a little bit of show and tell. I remember making a big poster, because I was a reception teacher at the time and so I made a colorful display to share with the rest of the people.

Helen's work must have impressed. One of the science consultants who had been working at the school alerted her to a new opportunity, a graduate program in math and science teaching at a local university, led by two academics, Doctor R and Doctor H. This program was being supported by both the local state department of education and the Catholic education office (see Figure 4.3). Helen was daunted but excited:

Figure 4.2. Helen's Initial Inquiry Network

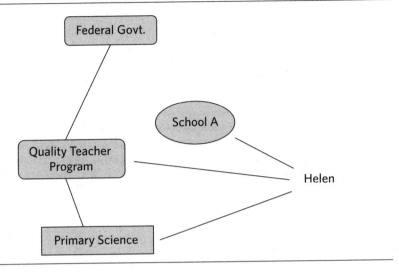

I hadn't studied for 13-odd years, close to, and goodness knows how I'd go doing things like essays! I knew I needed a lot of support in that particular vein, let alone doing the research part of it, although I'd gained a little bit of confidence the previous year. And so yeah, I was lucky and got into the graduate certificate.

The "little bit of confidence" that Helen had gained through her initial experience of practitioner inquiry on the topic of "questioning in science" gave her a sense that the graduate work would not be beyond her. So it proved and Helen completed the degree and the research component, deepening her understanding of mathematical and scientific learning in the junior primary years.

Greenhill Primary (School A in the figures) was a member of a cluster of local schools that collaborated for professional development. With her new graduate qualification and experience, Helen was offered the opportunity to lead some professional development in her curriculum specialization for the cluster. At one of the meetings, an issue of common interest arose with her cluster colleagues: At every school were some students whose high potential was not being sufficiently developed. Small rural schools have difficulty staffing specialist programs for gifted-and-talented students.

With interested cluster colleagues, Helen began to brainstorm ways of better resourcing schools to support mathematically and scientifically gifted students. They identified a funding source associated with a facility in the state capital that offered students the opportunity to take a weeklong course. Helen led the submission for a Students with High Intellectual Potential (SHIP) project, which was successful, and a group of 30 students

Figure 4.3. Helen Strengthens Her Inquiry Ties with the University

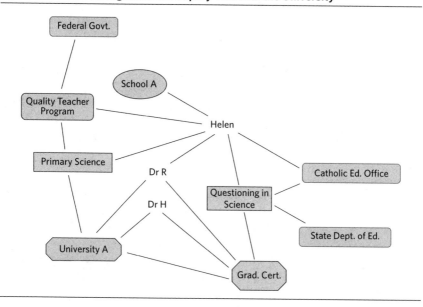

from across cluster schools traveled to the city and experienced an intensive program. Helen made sure to incorporate a research component (Gifted Students in Science) into this initiative so that she could generate knowledge about what the gifted students had gained from their time at the specialist center (see Figure 4.4.).

Working with the cluster was significant in Helen's career trajectory. Without aiming to be a leader, she found herself taking on increasing responsibility. Helen was encouraged by her principal to seek certification as an advanced skills teacher and then to take on acting leadership positions, first as deputy and then as principal. These acting leadership positions were in other cluster schools, which further strengthened Helen's networks while also enabling her to maintain a professional base at her home school. As can be seen from Figure 4.4, Helen's networks had become extensive and complex, more than we can do justice to in this brief career overview.

By this point, inquiry was not only integrated into Helen's professional practice but had become the foundation of her curriculum leadership:

> This [inquiry] gave me a bedrock. So that when I'm talking to other teachers about what they're doing, I've got a really good, strong basis to go from, and also understand where they're coming from. Because whenever I go into a school, and whenever I've got an application, to me the focus of leadership should always be on teaching, and therefore the learner, and all of the other stuff that comes onto leadership is secondary to that.

Figure 4.4. Helen Involves Her Regional Cluster in Inquiry

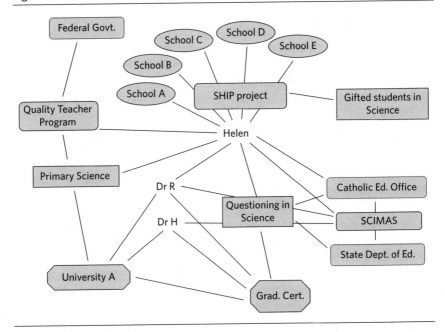

Though she had progressed to school leadership, Helen remained a passionate classroom exponent and indeed made this the center of her leadership. She valued inquiry precisely because it generated knowledge about the impacts of her pedagogical work and her students' engagement in learning. Inquiry also provided Helen with a basis for professional conversations with peers in and beyond her school. These dialogues sparked further questions and prompted joint initiatives and investigations—for example, an investigation into financial literacy that made a contribution to the state Science and Mathematics Strategy (SCIMAS).

The importance of leadership in fostering talent is highlighted in this case, echoing a study that tracked early career teachers identified as "highly promising" (Cameron & Lovett, 2015). Those teachers who, 9 years into practice, felt a strong sense of professional fulfillment all expressed appreciation for leaders who had "recognized their potential and . . . supported them to 'stretch and grow' within and outside their schools" (Cameron & Lovett, 2015, p. 155). For Helen's principal, inquiry projects were a key means by which talented teachers could be given scope to stretch and become leaders.

Russell: "Motivated to keep going"

Russell, a late-career professional, described himself as a person for whom reflection on practice was ingrained: "I've done reflective practice ever since I was 18 years old." Prior to enrolling in an inquiry-oriented graduate program, and during his subsequent studies, his career took him through a series of short-term appointments. As will be discussed in Chapter 5, teachers who succeed in tough assignments are at risk of being circulated through the system to solve the most intractable problems. Russell had worked in an educational service within the correctional system, at a school for students excluded from the mainstream, and as a behavior management coordinator in mainstream schools. In network terms, his ties with particular schools were weak (represented by the dotted line in Figure 4.5), whereas his commitment to reflection was a strong theme of continuity.

As Figure 4.5 shows, one of the school ties in Russell's network was strong. School D served students with a range of challenges, leading to their exclusion from the mainstream, as well as others whose parents sought alternative education. It was small and had a flexible, negotiated curriculum, and its teachers worked with considerable autonomy.

Russell's shift from everyday reflective practice to more formalized inquiry came about as a result of the Department of Education sponsoring a graduate course in the field of inclusive education (see Chapter 5). By this time, his contract at School D was up and he was now teaching in School E, a placement that involved a major responsibility for behavior management.

Figure 4.5. Russell's Network

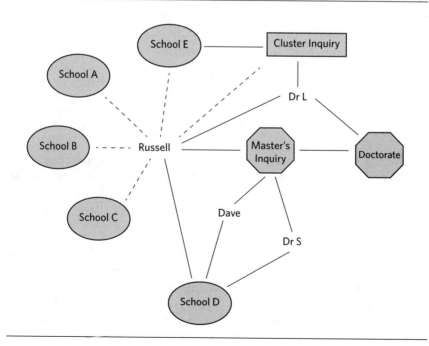

Russell was critical of the school's existing policy and was experiencing some difficulty convincing colleagues of the necessity for change.

When he entered the graduate program, Russell had a pleasant surprise. A colleague, Dave, who had also taught at School D, was enrolled. In addition, the lecturer, Dr S, had been a teacher at this school. All had prior ties that were renewed by their participation in the course (see Figure 4.5).

Perhaps because of his experience of transient employment, Russell was quite sensitive about whom he could work with most productively. He was frank in the interview about the process of judgment that he and his peers in the course used to determine which academics to approach for advice and support:

> The experience was particularly focused for me around who it was who I was having initial contact with from the uni, and that was Dr S and she was exceptionally good, and remained so through that program. . . . All of us had made assessments [of the academics]: "Don't want to be with that one. Want to be with that one."

Russell had held onto his professional values throughout a long, challenging career but had often felt isolated. He particularly appreciated that the inquiry community he joined was one that valued critique and welcomed different perspectives:

> It was a situation of being placed to feel confident that there was confirmation that the values that I held were worthwhile, that there were other places where they were seen to be worthwhile, and that my concepts could be analyzed.

It is noteworthy that Russell did not just seek confirmation but wanted his professional knowledge to be put to the test in an environment where others were also accepting of scrutiny. The experience was so professionally rewarding that Russell continued his studies with another graduate program, also inquiry-based.

During this time, he was also offered the opportunity to join a school cluster inquiry. There he met a familiar face, Dr L, who also taught in the initial graduate certificate course and was coleading the cluster inquiry. Interestingly, Dr L was one of the academics whom Russell had judged critically as someone who he did *not* want to work with. In this new context, however, Russell found Dr L's contribution constructive and his knowledge relevant. Indeed, this connection was so valuable that Russell sought out Dr L to be his advisor when he commenced doctoral studies (see Figure 4.5).

When he reflected on his experience, Russell highlighted his connections with the university as an institution that supported him as an inquiring practitioner. The line of continuity that Russell attempted to maintain, in terms of his orientation to reflection and critique, was strengthened through his membership in an inquiring community. Although members moved in and out of projects, and his relationships were subject to change, Russell continued to feel part of something beyond any particular site or project:

> It wasn't particularly any specific project so much as the contact with the university and the sense of there being resources which could support my way of gathering data and my way of examining issues. . . . While I was shifting from school to school to school, I was motivated to keep going, rather than feeling trapped by my own circumstances.

Alessandra: "I hate the word *network* but . . ."

Alessandra was a language teacher in a primary/elementary setting. Unlike Russell, her situation was relatively stable and she had experienced only one change of school, at her own initiation. Like Russell, she had experienced professional isolation over her career. This was in part because of her role as a language specialist, initially in a small school where there was no language department. However, she also described herself as having "always been a little bit innovative" and motivated by a desire to connect children's language learning to their learning in other curriculum areas and to their lives.

Her first experience of practitioner inquiry came about through a project on bilingualism that partnered schools in the Catholic education system with University A. Alessandra was excited to learn about the value of bilingual learning. She was keen to engage her colleagues in thinking about how to better utilize child and family language resources, especially as the school served a multicultural community (see Figure 4.6).

She was not prepared, however, for the strength of the negative reaction to her proposition that children might utilize languages other than English in their learning across the curriculum. She explained:

> I learned lots about language doing the bilingual program, but it's not good for staff morale. It just sort of . . . when you do something different, it always gets people upset sometimes in schools.

This made Alessandra very cautious about again attempting to bring her inquiry findings out of her own classroom. She was not deterred, however, from undertaking inquiry, and when an opportunity arose to join another inquiry cluster, she gained support from her principal to participate.

This inquiry was on the theme of visual literacy and was led by Dr D, an academic from University B and funded by the Catholic education system. This project involved a cluster of schools. However, in her retrospective interview Alessandra emphasized the significance of Dr D because this connection continued and was instrumental in creating further opportunities (see Figure 4.6).

Figure 4.6: Alessandra's Network

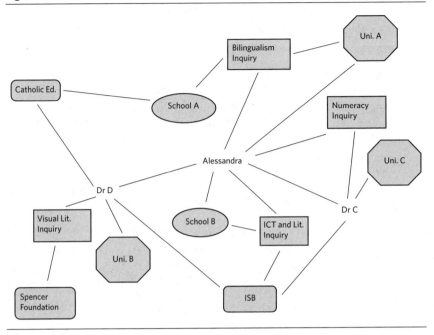

The next important step in Alessandra's career was her move to School B, which was a member of the Independent Schools system (consisting of schools not managed by either the state government or a major religious education provider). Alessandra was attracted to this school in part because staff members were encouraged to participate in reflective practice and inquiry. Through this school, Alessandra became involved in two further inquiry projects funded by the Independent Schools Board (ISB). During this time, Dr D also had an important career move, setting up an independent research consultancy, a role in which he led one of these inquiries, on the theme of ICTs and literacy. The other inquiry, on numeracy, was led by Dr C of University C, meaning that Alessandra's inquiry trajectory had included collaborations with all three major local universities (see Figure 4.6).

What she had learned through all these inquiries had contributed to Alessandra becoming a specialist in both language and literacy education, extending her expertise beyond her initial subject of Italian. She was now not only a seasoned classroom practitioner but also a highly experienced practitioner of teacher research. Alessandra began to find opportunities being offered that took her outside her school and into a wider arena. This included working on the design of a professional development program to implement a national language curriculum.

Reflecting on her career, Alessandra was struck by the importance of connections made through inquiry projects:

I hate the word *network*, but the network I had in Catholic education, those people have now moved on, some of them moved into the Independent Schools Board. Dr D is now running his own company so those people are in different areas now, and I guess they know what I can do and they've asked me to do all sorts of things.

It is interesting that Alessandra was reluctant to use the term *network* even though she acknowledged that it was the best word to describe what she, with others, had built over the years. We cannot go far in speculating about this hesitation, but it may reflect the individualistic nature of teacher identity, which is underpinned by a school and curriculum architecture based on the one-teacher-one-class model of accountability. Alessandra, who from the start had been somewhat transgressive of this model, paid a price for this at School A when colleagues stymied her attempt to collaboratively develop a cross-curriculum approach to language learning.

Despite challenges in operating as an inquiring classroom practitioner, Alessandra maintained her commitment to classroom practice as the center of her teacher identity. She was able to continue to do this while expanding her network through participation in inquiry projects. At School B she found a collegial environment that supported this activity and a leadership willing to give her time to take up new opportunities such as national curriculum development. Alessandra herself attributed her career success to hard work:

Without doing all this hard work in the past, and as I will have to continue in the future, all these good things would not have come.

This work could possibly be conceptualized in networking terms as a kind of energy that attracts connections and resources. Striking in Alessandra's inquiry network is the role of organizations in sponsoring teacher inquiry. These included two school systems, three universities, and an international funding body. Dr D has clearly been a pivotal network node through his strategic alliances with these organizations. Although we do not have Dr D's personal testimony, he might also be considered a kind of talent scout who had recognized Alessandra's capabilities, curiosity, and appetite for investigation.

CONCLUSION: CAREER PATHS FOR INQUIRING PRACTITIONERS

The networking model is particularly apt for describing the diverse and dynamic ways in which participation in practitioner inquiry impacted educators' careers. Some of these educators were active networkers before coming into inquiry, whereas others made the connection when they were recruited into an inquiry network. Particularly for those whose professional context had been characterized by isolation, this was a significant shift. Russell's isolation was a result of his transience; he was rarely at a school long enough to build strong collegial relationships. For Alessandra, isolation was a function of her specialist subject expertise, which was not shared with any colleagues at her small school. Joining inquiry networks gave these isolated individuals a sense of professional connection.

Of course, any professional grouping can do that, so why would we argue that inquiry is particularly significant? There is something about the purposeful, focused, and goal-oriented nature of inquiry that made the relationships particularly generative. Perhaps these were particularly purposive educators, like the "highly promising" group followed by Cameron and Lovett (2015). Being able to move in and out of inquiry groupings meant that their energy and intellectual curiosity could be channeled and made available for others. Networks live and grow because of the goods that circulate between connections (Horvat, Weininger, & Lareau, 2003; Vera & Schupp, 2006). In the accounts of Helen, Russell, and Alessandra, we see various kinds of goods that they accessed, produced, and circulated through their participation in inquiry networks. These included knowledge, advice, support, and resources relevant to their professional goals.

Organizations were important in providing the infrastructure and resources that enabled many of the inquiry and professional networks to be initiated and to continue functioning. Each of the network profiles discussed above demonstrates this. Universities featured prominently in bringing academic researchers and subject specialists into contact with teachers through inquiry communities and in providing accreditation through graduate programs that integrated inquiry. Federal and state governments and nonstate systems also funded and resourced inquiry programs. When educators joined inquiries, they connected with these larger networks, as well as with individuals who had connections to these networks. These individuals could be considered "Diverse Professional Allies" in Baker-Doyle's (2011) terms. Such alliances could result in further opportunities being made available to educators. A case in point is the role of Dr D in Alessandra's professional network. This entrepreneurial individual had connections with two major systems (the Catholic and independent school systems) as well as a federal curriculum authority and a university. Alessandra, for her part, provided Dr D with a continuing connection to the world of classroom practice.

Although influence and reputation can develop through individual interactions, there has also been a move toward formalizing the concept of teacher leadership (also called curriculum leadership) as a distinct role different from school management. Referring to the "the growing need for teachers to accept responsibility beyond the classroom," Dawson (2011, p. 18) argues that professional development programs should address this need directly. In a study of teacher attitudes toward curriculum leadership, he found that most classroom teachers had "developed tacit understand-ings of leadership that were associated with position, authority, and status" (Dawson, 2011, p. 21). It was necessary to challenge this view in order to support teachers to see leadership as complementary to, rather than at odds with, their commitment to classroom-based effective teaching.

The concept of lead teacher or curriculum leadership applies to many of the IPI teachers. That is, while maintaining their commitment to classroom practice as the core of their professional identity, over time they assumed responsibility for professional roles outside the classroom. They began to be viewed by peers as leaders and to actively initiate and drive projects. The role of lead teacher is codified in the Australian national professional stan-dards for teachers (Australian Institute for Teaching and School Leadership [AITSL], 2011). These standards structure a developmental pathway for teachers from the graduate stage through proficient and highly proficient and culminating in lead teacher status. It is significant that the ability to undertake research is included as a competency for lead teachers. This stan-dard appears in the Professional Engagement category:

> Initiate collaborative relationships to expand professional learning opportuni-ties, engage in research, and provide quality opportunities and placements for pre-service teachers. (AITSL, 2011, p. 18)

The lead teacher is also expected to be a critical user of research and to lead colleagues in

> professional dialogue with the school and/or professional learning network(s) that is informed by feedback, analysis of current research and practice to im-prove the educational outcomes of students. (AITSL, 2011, p. 18)

School leaders have a responsibility to manage staff performance with reference to these standards. Although performance management has been critiqued as a technique of neoliberal regulation (Liew, 2012), it can also motivate leaders to support the development of teachers from proficiency to leadership. Toward this end, supporting teachers in undertaking inquiry may provide leaders with evidence of their suitability for leadership, while also providing a means to address school improvement goals.

Helen's trajectory can be seen as an example of this. Her principal en-listed the school in the Quality Teacher Project and, based on Helen's per-formance in this project, supported her enrollment in a graduate course. Helen's time spent on cluster activities and grant writing were also sup-ported with the allocation of time. Helen's opportunities were scaled ac-cording to her developing scope of expertise, beginning with her own class, to the school, and then to the cluster. In this process, inquiry was a central mechanism that enabled Helen to further her learning, generate evidence of effectiveness as a practitioner, and expand her professional network.

Teacher research is not uniformly recognized in codifications of standards. In 2013, the OECD published a survey of competency frameworks from 12 jurisdictions, including countries in Europe, Latin America, the Asia Pacific, and also two states within the United States (Texas and California). Standards fell into three categories: (1) Disciplinary Knowledge, (2) Pedagogic Practice, and (3) Values and Professional Teaching Practice. The greatest emphasis was found in the second category with a focus on planning, implementing, and assessing teaching and learning. There was also a consistent emphasis on teachers developing "higher order critical thinking skills" and "knowing how to use ICT for learning" (Centre for Study of Policies and Practices in Education [CEPPE], 2013, p. 35).

Under Values and Professional Teaching Practice were competencies that relate to the educator as a learner. Most of the standards include reflective practice and commitment to professional learning. However, the terms *research* and *inquiry* did not make a direct appearance in this overview of teaching standards. In practice, these standards could be met in a range of ways, including the traditional top-down professional development (PD) session in which the teacher takes a relatively passive role.

However, standards for principals did include competencies directly associated with inquiry. These included the ability to analyze information for decisionmaking aimed at making improvement, to monitor learning using data, and to incorporate "inputs from research" into leadership practices (CEPPE, 2013, p. 54). It is interesting that reflection on practice appears in 11 out of 12 teacher competency frameworks but in only two of the principal frameworks. This implies that in the trajectory from teacher to leader, reflective practice is expected to be replaced with a more systematic and less personal approach to analysis and decisionmaking. From this perspective, participation in practitioner inquiry, even when not specifically recognized in leadership standards, can potentially support a leadership trajectory by helping teachers gain skill in analysis and the use of research.

Whether or not inquiry is explicitly named in codifications of teacher professionalism, the general picture of an educator who is active, critical, collaborative, self-reflective, and committed to improvement is reinforced by standards frameworks. This potentially supports teachers and leaders who wish to use inquiry to evidence these qualities. Inquiry has become a key means by which teachers and educational leaders can strengthen their professional knowledge, practice, and engagement, and through which they can generate evidence that they are doing so.

PART II

IMPACTFUL INQUIRY PROJECTS

CHAPTER 5

The Inclusive Education Project
Inquiry as Critical Action Toward More Inclusive Schools

The Impact of Practitioner Inquiry investigation asked participants to nominate what they considered to be the "most impactful" inquiry they had experienced. The Inclusive Education Project was selected by some as their "most impactful" inquiry. This project aimed to make a change in the way that students with a range of differences were thought about and educated. The project's scope encompassed students whose differences could in any way present difficulties for the system in terms of ensuring participation, access to opportunities, and achievement. Thus, differences of ability, race, language, behavior, and social class were all considered in relation to the including and excluding processes of education.

The project was initiated and strongly supported by a senior manager in a state education unit responsible for the provision of support to students with a range of special needs. This manager believed strongly in the importance of advanced study and regularly funded teachers to undertake graduate programs. These programs had previously been in relation to specific disability categories such as autism and hearing impairment. The decision to shift some PD resources away from specialist areas and into inclusive education was a significant move. It reflected a drive to engage the system as a whole in addressing both barriers and enablers to student participation and achievement. This project brought together 25 educators from diverse sites of practice, including mainstream schools, specialist schools and units, and from early childhood through high school. The group represented classroom teachers, school leaders, and administrators. It was hoped that the project would have a ripple effect throughout the system.

The program was designed from the outset to be inquiry focused. This reflected in part the influence of the inclusive education movement in the United Kingdom, which had made school-based inquiry a key strategy in challenging practices of exclusion and working toward more inclusive schools. Among school reform movements, inclusive education has been distinguished by unusually strong support for teacher research as a central strategy in policy implementation. This is particularly the case in the United Kingdom, where a school research network was established in 2000 by the government's Economic and Social Research Council's Teaching and Learning Research program (Howes, Booth, Dyson, & Frankham, 2005; Howes, Frankham, Ainscow, & Farrell, 2004). This network of 24 schools across three local government areas was established to address barriers to the participation and learning of students with special educational needs, who had been included in mainstream schools under the inclusive education policy. The network's action research program was intended to generate knowledge for the whole education system, with the aim of improving the participation and achievement of these students.

A key tool in the United Kingdom–based inclusion research movement was, and continues to be, the Index for Inclusion (Booth & Ainscow, 2000). This tool is a form of survey that can be used by schools in analyzing the existing conditions for inclusion, planning for change, and evaluating the success of interventions. The index has three major sections: (1) creating inclusive cultures; (2) producing inclusive policies; and (3) evolving inclusive practices. As this sequence suggests, an inclusive school culture is viewed as the foundation on which policy and practice rest. Each of these sections has a list of themes and indicators. For instance, under "creating inclusive cultures," the first theme is "building community," and the indicators listed are as follows: Everyone is made to feel welcome; students help each other; staff collaborates with one another; and staff and students treat one another with respect (Booth & Ainscow, 2000).

The Index for Inclusion is based on the social model of disability (Oliver, 1990, 2013), which argues that disabilities are best thought of as contextual impairments. That is, whether a personal characteristic serves as an ability or disability is strongly influenced by the environment. This view has been significant in shifting research on inclusion into schools. In contrast, knowledge production in the field of special education has been the province of psychological and medical research. For schools, coming to grips with the social model of disability has meant focusing attention on how aspects of schooling (spatial, social, cultural, and curricular) might function to both enable and disable.

The inquiry movement associated with this inclusion model strongly emphasized collaboration and collective reflection as a means of producing change at the level of school cultures. Within this process, differences were to be acknowledged and worked with, rather than smoothed over to achieve consensus. Research leaders argued:

> [S]ocial learning is effectively facilitated through a research-like orientation, whereby differing perspectives are encountered rather than ignored or overlooked, in a process which quite explicitly sets out to raise questions and disturb preconceptions. (Howes et al., 2005, p. 135)

This orientation was reflected in the Inclusive Education Project's deliberate bringing together of educators with different perspectives arising from their different histories, sites of practice, and roles. The full-year program involved two strands that ran concurrently: an inclusive education strand and a practitioner inquiry strand. As the educators were encountering theories and research related to inclusion, they were also learning about and undertaking practitioner inquiry.

Reports on inquiry often focus on fieldwork and subsequent outcomes. In this chapter, we devote considerable attention to activities that might be considered preparations for inquiry but that we argue were of vital importance in enabling educators to enter the complex field of inclusion as inquirers. The project team spent the first two terms of the school year reading, reflecting, and undertaking various analytical tasks. This period enabled us to explore the complex terrain of inclusion and exclusion and to air different perspectives on problems, opportunities, and possible ways forward. These activities involved analysis of educators' environments, beliefs, and practices, and thus were also forms of inquiry. Sharing their analyses in the collective prompted extended discussion of the complexities involved in working toward the goal of inclusion and enabled educators to shape the action component of their inquiries with a greater understanding of these complexities.

INTERROGATING INCLUSION AND EXCLUSION

The first stage of the project was characterized by intense reading, reflection, dialogue, and debate. The aim of these discussions was not to achieve a consensus in the group but, rather, to more fully understand the diversity of perspectives and the complexity of the issues. We considered perspectives from psychology, neuropsychology, special education, the mainstream, disability studies, and people who identified as individuals with a disability. For instance, a textbook on autism was juxtaposed with a satirical website on so-called "neurotypical syndrome" set up by a disability activist.

We quickly found ourselves confronting some of the key debates in the field. Should students be assisted to fit the mainstream and should this be seen as in their best interest? Or should schools be the leaders in social change aimed at changing the world into which our students will graduate? Was a specialist service catering only to students with disabilities reinforcing social exclusion? Or might the sense of belonging experienced in such contexts be a more genuine experience of inclusion than social isolation in the mainstream? The group included those who worked with students in specialist settings separate from the mainstream, including a school for students with multiple and severe disabilities and a school for students whose challenging behavior had disqualified them from mainstream education.

There were also teachers and principals who worked in a mainstream setting, some of whom strongly believed that all students should be educated in such settings. The range of organizational contexts, roles, and curriculum areas across the team created a rich resource of experiences and interpretive frames.

The figure of the "extreme case" came up regularly in these conversations, evoking the student for whom mainstream settings did not (and some argued could not) work. Siobhan, a school principal, said she did not want to exclude such pupils; however, it was the only way to attract resources: "You have to go through exclusion to prove there's a problem." Ruth, who worked in a specialist school, argued that the mainstream needed to change to be capable of offering a supportive environment for so-called challenging students: "We're talking about modifying the student behaviors, but it should be about the teachers."

Sharing reflections of our own histories of practice was an important strategy in raising awareness of our resources and challenges. This helped practitioners consider how they may be able to act as agents for change. We came to the realization that many of our number not only worked with marginalized students, but also were marginalized themselves. This was made strikingly evident by the educators' reflections on their own histories in practice. Some of the teachers had special education training and had intended to follow careers working with special-needs students. For these teachers, it made sense to be working with a "special" class or in withdrawal situations. Among this group were those who had moved into leadership and administrative roles. Sebastian, for instance, was a district coordinator of disability services whose role involved finding appropriate placements and supports for students. Members of this group had a strong sense of their professional knowledge base but were less sure about the possibilities for influencing the mainstream.

A second group had no specialist training. Many had found themselves becoming unofficial "specialists" by virtue of their junior status, willingness, or need for a job. In other words, these tough assignments were often meted out to those who had the least right to say no. In Nigel's first appointment as a newly minted teacher, he was sent to a regional town in which the majority of residents were low income or unemployed. Like many first-year teachers, he did not get a permanent job straight away. In this situation, teachers are on probation and their reports can help determine whether they get more work. He needed to succeed:

> I was on a contract and I inherited a special-needs class. That class was in a transportable building right at the back of the school. The principal said, "Go in there and make them happy." He didn't seem too worried what I did in there. So I worked to get those kids back to school.

Dave thought he was being assigned to a specialist school for children with disabilities but instead found himself in a school that catered exclusively to "disruptive and disinclined" students:

What a shock! As music teacher my role was just to keep them in there, you know, stop them from actually running away. But after a while I realized there was a massive potential for kids that were disadvantaged.

As these stories show, schools have ways of quarantining difficult students, those who either cannot or will not engage with the academic curriculum. In too many schools, these students were put out of sight and out of mind. Without support, only exceptional practitioners could survive in these challenging contexts. Some even thrived, and these individuals found themselves with many more such assignments.

Such a career path was often not as stable or predictable as that for more mainstream teachers. Many members of the group spoke of going from contract to contract, always finding themselves with difficult classes or in challenging schools. Jennifer had worked for 21 years, 19 of them as a contract teacher without a permanent appointment. Russell, after 10 years at an alternative school for challenging students and an additional 5 in a juvenile detention center, was only able to get short-term contracts in regular schools. Normative assumptions, structures, and practices advantage students who fit the norm and also position the teachers of those students in the center of the mainstream. As Broderick and colleagues (2012) put it:

The binary majoritarian narrative about abled/disabled or normal/abnormal students . . . is inextricably intertwined with the narrative that there are different "kinds" of teachers best suited to be a teacher to each "kind" of student. (p. 832)

One of the aims of the Inclusive Education Project was to challenge the categorization of students into groups. Applying membership categories such as "at-risk," "disabled," or "disadvantaged" can have the effect of suggesting that all people in a particular category face the same challenges (Armstrong, 2001; Reid, Maag, & Vasa, 1993). This can draw attention away from the specificities of a person's strengths, resources, and obstacles, all of which are important elements in inclusive education. Having worked with students whose differences had excluded them in various ways, we understood their potential, talents, and aspirations. Thus, we all took the view that "[d]iverse human identities including disability, race, gender, class, sexual orientation, and religion are accepted without judgment, ranking, or pathologization" (Danforth & Jones, 2015, p. 16).

THE DIMENSIONS OF DIVERSITY CASE STUDY

As well as reading and discussion, the team undertook a number of activities in the preparatory stage of the project. One that proved to be generative was the Dimensions of Diversity case study. This case study was organized with the aid of a tool. A concept map was based on a critical language awareness exercise used by South African critical sociolinguist Hilary Janks (1993) in her teacher education work. The teacher inquirers were also provided with a set of readings chosen to highlight aspects of diversity as experienced by students and their families in different contexts (e.g., Benjamin, 2001; Diniz & Usmani, 2003; Jule, 2004).

This tool (see Figure 5.1) encourages the black-box term *diversity* to be opened up by considering all the facets of social identity for students. It guides educators in developing a fuller appreciation of the social and personal complexities of student lives.

In relation to the goals of inclusive education, this tool achieves two purposes: First, it challenges the use of simple binary categorizations for learners (for example, able/disabled, normal/different, achieving/failing) by demonstrating that all individuals have multiple domains of identity that might impact on their learning and participation. Second, it opens up the question of inclusion to a finer-grained analysis, as educators consider inclusions and exclusions that are relevant to multiple dimensions of difference. For instance, a student might be included in some ways on the

Figure 5.1. Dimensions of Diversity Tool

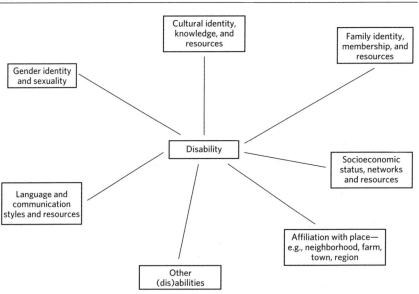

basis of ability but excluded on the basis of gender or race. Below, we see how two members of the group used this tool to develop new layers of understanding regarding their students and how they drew on their reading as part of this task.

Shanti

Katherine selected Shanti, an 18-year-old student with whom she worked in a special education class in a mainstream high school who had an intellectual disability. She was concerned that Shanti's reliance on support was a barrier to her achieving progress. Katherine described Shanti as having a "shy demeanor and inability to do any tasks without peer or teacher intervention" (Fisher, 2005).

Using the Dimensions of Diversity diagram (Figure 5.1) Katherine identified cultural and family identity, educational background, and ESL status as aspects of Shanti's experience. This prompted her to consider the possible impact of Shanti's experiences on her participation in school, something she had not previously considered.

Katherine found the work of Shereen Benjamin (2002) particularly helpful in thinking about how the experience of diversity might be impacting Shanti. Benjamin researched her own practice as a learning support educator in a multicultural single-sex London school. She identified racialized differences in the ways that learning disabled students from particular cultural backgrounds were positioned and positioned themselves. Benjamin noted that girls of East Asian heritage were seen as "sweet little girls," a designation that legitimized intensive help-seeking. In contrast, Afro-Caribbean girls took up the identities of "bad girls" whose difficulties were seen, in part, as a result of defiance and disinterest.

Like the "sweet little girls" in Benjamin's school, Shanti's dependence had been considered simply a feature of her disability until critical reflection highlighted the complex interplay of difference. The Dimensions of Diversity activity, and the example of Benjamin's analysis, enabled an appreciation of other ways in which difference might be having an impact. Gender, which Katherine had not initially included as an aspect of Shanti's experience, was now given recognition. Concluding her case study, Katherine wrote:

> Based on an understanding of Shanti's background, it seemed that her development of this pattern of behavior . . . might involve several different "dimensions of diversity": that it was a coping strategy potentially encompassing issues of gender, cultural background and transience. (Fisher, 2005)

The role of transience took on a significance that Katherine had not initially considered. Shanti had been adopted at the age of 7 from an orphanage in an Asian country. Her education had taken place in a number of settings, all very different from one another. Although Shanti now appeared to be settled and happy living with her Anglo-Australian adoptive parents, Katherine began to appreciate that adapting to so many educational and social contexts was challenging. Help-seeking now seemed an understandable survival skill rather than a deficit.

Tapu

Ruth chose to consider Tapu, one of her students in Queens Park School, a specialist facility for students with multiple and severe disabilities. She initially described him as "a boy who is 8 years old with hydrocephalus who has hemiplegic spasticity and intellectual global delay." This description highlights neurological abnormality as the focus of Tapu's difference. Ruth's reason for concern was Tapu's lack of motivation to communicate or participate in learning; he spent most of his time "just sitting."

It had been clear that within Ruth's setting, the question of students' cultural and social contexts rarely came up in team discussions. Thinking about her context in terms of the sociocultural aspects of inclusion was a new direction for Ruth. She was aware that Tapu's family had originally come from a Pacific island; however, she knew little more than that and was interested to explore these other dimensions of difference.

Ruth already had a good relationship with Tapu's mother as a trusted informant on her son's well-being and health. Ruth now asked different kinds of questions about the family's cultural identity and Tapu's place within his family and community. Learning that the whole family loved traditional island music, Ruth asked for some recordings. She began to associate familiar songs with the visual symbols that Tapu used for communication. After some repetition, Tapu began to choose symbols much more readily and frequently than before.

Ruth shared video recordings of Tapu's school-based activities with his family and audio-recorded their conversations. Transcripts of some of these conversations were included in her case study. At one point, Tapu's mother, Susan, noted a moment at school when Tapu began hitting the base of a shiny tin while staring intently at it, an activity that Ruth had not noted as particularly meaningful. Susan observed: "It's like he's playing the drums and watching himself play in his reflection." She told Ruth that Tapu attended drumming classes taught by his father: "Tapu does the whole thing . . . he just is in heaven." Following this exchange, Ruth began to notice more nuances in Tapu's actions: "He will turn the tin sideways to get sound when he hits it on the edge . . . he alters the tone of the drum." Susan confirmed that this technique was used by drummers like Tapu's father.

Through learning about the family's cultural practices, Ruth was able to expand her interpretive resources for understanding Tapu and for engaging him in learning. This gave new meaning to the concept of inclusive education.

INQUIRERS AS CHANGE AGENTS

The next stage of the preparatory program involved the educators in working with others at their school sites to explore issues of inclusion and exclusion. The project's mission was broader than just changing an individual's practice. Whether by intention or from necessity, all of these educators had gained a strong commitment to marginalized students and a faith in what Dave referred as their "massive potential." The goal of inclusion, though, is inherently about changing schools and systems. Many of the educators were frustrated that their colleagues did not necessarily share their beliefs. Tom, a school principal, said:

> I have always worked in disadvantaged schools. I know the potential of these kids. But what I'm thinking about now is, how much can we influence teachers? How much can we influence the community?

These practitioners were encouraged to consider themselves change agents. To facilitate this process, the educators were encouraged to engage colleagues in analyzing, questioning, and discussing inclusionary and exclusionary aspects of education at their sites. Tools such as the Index for Inclusion and the Dimensions of Diversity provided them with ways to open up discussion. Members of the team variously gave presentations, formed working groups, or teamed with a partner to undertake collaborative inquiry. For some, this was the aspect that contributed most to the inquiry's impact.

This was particularly so for those whose specialist role had contributed to their isolation. Bonnie, for instance, was the special education coordinator at a high school with a diverse student population. In this role, she was considered the representative of these students and was granted a voice on issues related to their special needs. However, she had never attempted to intervene in issues of mainstream classroom practice or school climate. Shifting the focus from special-needs provision to inclusive education opened up a space for Bonnie to engage her colleagues differently.

A SPECIALIST TEACHER OPENS DISCUSSION ON INCLUSIVE EDUCATION

In Bonnie's school, educational disadvantage was not limited to students with identified special educational needs. Three-quarters of the students enrolled qualified for federal government subsidies because of economic disadvantage and one-third had a language other than English as their mother tongue. This was a challenging school, and Bonnie was particularly concerned to involve the "dedicated and hardworking" teaching staff in a manner that was constructive and acknowledged success, and was also frank and open. This was essential to her own inquiry work, as her colleagues'

perspectives on inclusion would impact their willingness to participate and
to act on the findings.

Bonnie sought her principal's approval to devote a staff meeting to inclusion. She prepared by writing a brief preparatory article that, though
based on scholarly reading, was clear, concise, and upbeat. The meeting
began with guided self-reflection. Bonnie asked the teachers to remember
their own experience of schooling and ways in which they felt included and
excluded. She asked them to "jot down three points that would have made
your schooling more inclusive" and gave them permission to be "fanciful."
She showed them a quotation from an article reporting parents' frustrating
experiences in finding an inclusive educational setting for a child with a disability (Purdue, Ballard, & Macarthur, 2001). She asked them to imagine
that they were the parent: "What would you like to see done for your child?
How would you feel when the school does its best to include your child?"

Bonnie then opened up the question of inclusion more broadly, framing
it as about catering to differences of all kinds, by showing the slide displayed
in Figure 5.2 below.

Bonnie adapted the Dimensions of Diversity activity to organize her
staff's analysis of inclusion at their school and to extend their thinking beyond the special education model of support for "disabled" students. After discussion, she presented a summary of points arising from research on

Figure 5.2. Slide from Bonnie's Presentation to Colleagues

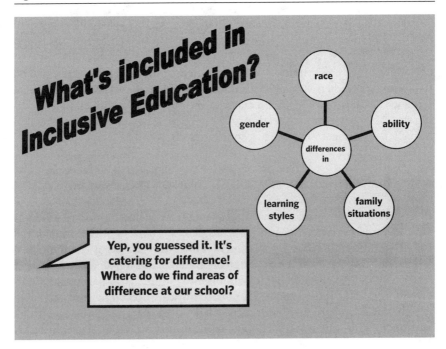

factors enabling and challenging inclusion. After an offer to provide further readings and a follow-up session, time was up.

The process would be ongoing. In her report, Bonnie wrote: "I have realized it has the potential to drive discussion and reflection for a period far longer than a regular training and development segment." Had Bonnie conducted an analysis on her school and then presented it to her colleagues as a fait accompli, the result would have been alienating and counterproductive. Through the carefully designed workshop, she was able to involve the school staff in beginning an analysis of inclusion and exclusion at their site without defensiveness.

UNDERTAKING INQUIRY

Following this period of reading, reflection, exploration, and discussion, it was time for the Inclusive Education Project team to design and undertake their inquiries, which were done individually but, in many cases, involved others at the educators' sites. For many, this was the first time they had designed and carried out an inquiry involving data collection, analysis, and reporting. Their preparatory activities showed them the complexity of the terrain they were entering. In many ways, they felt they were still at the beginning of understanding inclusion and exclusion and how these played out in their schools. Many had assumed that they would undertake an intervention. However, one of the outcomes of this extended period of exploration is that many of the teachers decided to undertake more exploratory inquiries, hoping to generate knowledge that would contribute to decisions about what form of intervention might be most promising.

Another significant shift was in the direction of collaborative inquiry. Educators began to see peers and, in some cases, students as co-inquirers, whereas previously they had seen themselves as studying others rather than inquiring with them. With this shift came the possibility that the inquiry question itself might be open to negotiation and change. In some cases, this happened in the course of doing the inquiry. Tom, a primary school principal, reflected on this process:

> The original research question was around: *What is more effective, to have in-class or out-of-class* [support]? But what came out of that was . . . the realization that educating parents as to what we were doing and why we were doing that, and gaining their support as well was really important. So it was like it came out of the question; it wasn't the original question.

This realization meant that Tom redesigned his inquiry to be inclusive of parents when originally he had expected to be generating evidence to "prove" one way or the other which of two support models "worked." Rather than presenting this evidence to parents as a way to shortcut their possible objections, he recognized that teachers did not really know what parents understood, believed, or wished for when their children were struggling. Discovering this was now seen as valuable in itself and as a way of assisting teachers in working constructively with parents to find the most promising form of support for each student.

Another characteristic of these inquiries was that the question, rationale, and analysis were generally deeply informed by reading. As we have shown, this was a characteristic of the activities that preceded the inquiry proper. In working through these exercises, the educators became used to connecting their questions, analyses, and explanations with those of a discourse community. This was particularly important for Dave, whose inquiry is described in detail below. Following this, we will discuss another example of practitioner inquiry into inclusive education, that of Chris Boulter, who pursued his inquiry at the doctoral level.

Investigating Indigenous Students' Identities Through Video

Dave was principal at Seekworthy, a school for urban Aboriginal students. This school had been established as a result of advocacy by members of the traditional landowners of that area. The history of Aboriginal people after their lands were settled by European colonists has been one of dispossession, dispersal, survival, and renewal. Indigenous people were displaced from their lands on what is now the city and withdrew to camps that later became rural towns and, later still, suburbs (Amery, 2014). Across Australia, Indigenous children's educational participation and achievement has lagged far behind their counterparts' because of poverty, social disruption, racism, poor services in remote locations, and having English as a second or third language (McInerney, 2005). Establishing Seekworthy was an important step in renewing heritage and language as well as engaging Aboriginal students in education.

A non-Indigenous self-identified "whitefella," Dave had a history of working in alternative education and had taught at "Urban Community School" with Russell. Dave was greatly concerned with the question of inclusivity. He saw it from two perspectives simultaneously. On the one hand, he was happy that Seekworthy functioned as a welcoming, safe environment that kept Aboriginal youth connected with learning when they might otherwise become truants. On the other, he wondered about how connected Seekworthy was with the broader community and whether its separation from the mainstream might disadvantage its students. He worried that in emphasizing belonging, teachers might be satisfied with lesser degrees of challenge than students would confront in mainstream schools. Students' attendance was spasmodic, and they did not necessarily complete tasks. He wondered how it might be possible to engage more meaningfully with the local Indigenous community, while at the same time offering authentic educational challenges to students.

Dave decided to focus his inquiry on his students' engagement in media production with an emphasis on how they used video to explore issues of identity and belonging at school. The use of video had a successful history at Seekworthy, where a specialist media teacher taught production skills. Two of the students were studying media studies for their senior secondary certificate. They were to be the first two students ever to graduate from Seekworthy with a senior high school qualification. The student cohort had already participated in making a health promotion video with peers in regional schools.

To date, media projects had focused on specific subject-area learning and on the goal of creating high-quality media products. Dave decided to learn more about the process through which students engaged in creating a video. He decided to ask students to work with some video footage they had already recorded and to edit it into a new media product. During this process, he planned to video the students at work, interview individuals, and collect artifacts.

Earlier, the media students had produced a set of video interviews aimed at exploring perspectives on Seekworthy. They interviewed three categories of participants: cultural elders who had been instrumental in establishing the school, past students, and present students. The interviews had not yet been edited and existed only as raw footage. Because the theme of the video collection was so closely related to the meaning of Seekworthy as a place for Indigenous students, Dave could see an exciting opportunity to build new understandings of his students' personal and collective identities. He hoped this inquiry would contribute to his critical reflection on the meaning of inclusion and exclusion for Indigenous students in general and those at Seekworthy in particular.

Dave sought readings that would assist him in this task. He found Giroux's (1998) book *Channel Surfing: Racism, the Media, and the Destruction of Today's Youth*. One quote in particular resonated and was included in his report:

> Educationally and politically, young people need to be given the opportunity to narrate themselves, to speak from the actual places where their experiences and daily lives are shaped and mediated. (Giroux, 1998, p. 31)

He also located the work of a local Indigenous scholar (Kickett-Tucker, 1998) who offered important insights into the educational experiences of urban Aboriginal children. This assisted Dave in understanding the impact of racism and exclusion on children's mainstream schooling experiences. He was particularly excited to find an analysis of the use of video for "re-presenting culture" by First Nations youth in Canada (Riecken et al., 2006).

As Dave analyzed the videos of his students editing their video, he paid attention to the segments they identified for selection in the final product. These were considered significant as representations of the students' collective identity as students of Seekworthy. He listened to their talk to gain insights into why they chose these particular segments. He compared the group sessions with recordings of individual editing sessions. He then looked at the final 5-minute video as the product of a complex process of negotiation by his students, culminating in a shared vision of how they wished to represent Seekworthy to peers, the local Aboriginal community, and wider Indigenous and non-Indigenous audiences.

Here are three of the interview quotes that made it through the students' rigorous selection process and into the final video:

> We suddenly realized that there was racism coming from the teachers, and we said that if our kids have to face this, then what's in the future for them? Nothing. (Elder)

> I think you need schools where kids can feel it's part of them. It's got an Aboriginal name and they feel they belong. (Elder)

> We belong here. Be proud of your culture, keep going strong, and do whatever it is that makes you feel good. (Past student)

In discussing the first quote, Seekworthy students who had spent time in the mainstream spoke of their experiences of racism and feelings of exclusion. They contrasted this to the strong feeling of belonging they experienced at Seekworthy and articulated what made them "feel good" about being there.

Listening to the audio and considering these choices prompted Dave to reconsider some of his concerns about the school being a soft option. In a discussion with peers, he had earlier described students' claims for personal attention and his worry that they were becoming dependent on high levels of personal support as "a bit precious." He gave as an example students popping into his office to "have a yarn." Though he valued the interaction, was this just work avoidance? Students' comments while editing gave him a new insight into the integral relationship of emotional support, practical help, and the possibility of educational achievement:

> They help us with our other problems while we come to school.

> You get a warm welcome.

> We come here, and everyone knows where we are coming from. They treat us like we are their own kids.

In his report, Dave wrote:

> Students were passionate about the extra levels of support that they
> required and clearly identified ways in which they believed the school
> processes addressed these needs. This support also seems to impact on
> their feelings about school identity, belonging, and the staff within the
> organization.

Here, Dave represented his students as strong self-advocates and credited them with knowing what they needed to succeed at school. Although
he had always believed in providing support, he could now see that his
students, too, saw this as an investment in their futures. Their selections in
editing the video and their discussion of the points raised in the recorded
interviews were vital resources for Dave in coming to a better understanding
of what inclusion looked like in his context.

Dave's inquiry reflected the aims and approach of the Inclusive Education Project in the following ways:

- It focused attention on multiple forms of inclusion and exclusion at
  an educational site.
- It took a strength-based approach to learners.
- It was reflexive, involving the educator in scrutinizing his own
  assumptions and practices.
- Through analysis of artifacts of learning, it generated evidence of
  inclusionary and/or exclusionary impacts of particular teaching/
  learning practices.
- It was deeply informed by reading the work of educators and
  researchers in inclusive education or a related field.

Investigating Teachers' Experiences of Inclusion

Chris was a Canadian elementary school principal. A nagging feeling
about the gap between inclusion policy and inclusion practice prompted
him to enroll in a doctoral program. (Because Chris's dissertation is in
the public domain, his actual name has been used.) Though his story is
not from the Inclusive Education Project, we tell it here as an example
of how an educator can take a practitioner inquiry approach to research
at the doctoral level, maintaining a focus on practice throughout the
process.

Chris wanted to research from within the system and gain a platform
for exposing problems that he believed were being glossed over in the
drive to present inclusion as a success story. He insisted from the start that
he did not want to leave the system to become a university academic and,
indeed, he stayed within his school throughout the doctorate and beyond.

Interestingly, Chris's account of how he came to be working in this field was very similar to that of the Inclusive Education Project teachers:

> My first teaching position . . . involved working with students who were deemed unfit for the regular classroom, either through academic concerns, behavior, or both. I had a multi-age group that would be with me all day in a segregated setting. It was called "Jr. Alternate," and was completely separate from the regular stream. My role was to do what I could with the students put in my room, and my recollection was that there were minimal expectations in regards to curriculum delivery. (Boulter, 2010, p. 9)

From surviving this assignment, Chris soon found himself allocated to the role of resource teacher, which, following the introduction of an inclusion policy in his province, made him responsible for managing learning programs for the "included" students. These students were now supposed to be learning alongside their peers in mainstream classes, supported by accommodations and in-class paraprofessionals.

However, rather than inclusive teaching, Chris saw the continuation of past practices of students being withdrawn from classes to work with specialist teachers away from their peers. Teachers were resisting the inclusion of these students, and some sought support from their union for claims of unfair treatment of themselves as professionals. Chris found himself being treated by peers as someone whose presumed specialist skills would be best employed working with struggling students outside the mainstream class. Seeing how some of the students fared in the mainstream, he wondered if that might be true.

Chris's inquiry method was simple enough. He invited six teachers on his staff to participate in a series of two semi-structured interviews exploring their beliefs, experiences, and wishes related to the inclusion of students with learning disabilities in their classes. However, the project was complex personally, politically, and ethically. As a practitioner inquirer, Chris was embedded in the context he was researching, and he was keenly aware of the importance of critical self-reflection throughout the process. He writes:

> I was not just reading policy and listening to how teachers represented themselves and others within it. The knowledge about the localized context was not always external to me; I had lived (and continue to live) the conditions teachers spoke of. (Boulter, 2010, p. 10)

Looking for a way to see his situation in a new light, Chris began reading in the field of critical disability studies. He came across the book *Reading and Writing Disability Differently: The Textured Life of Embodiment* by Tanya Titchkosky (2007). The author argues that disability is not something an individual has; it is something that a society *makes*, meaning everyone is implicated. She modeled a reflexive analysis considering herself as subject to, and able to reinforce or challenge, definitions of normality that exclude those outside the terms of the definition. Titchkowsky's work also showed Chris how policy and other kinds of texts can be interrogated for their normalizing effects.

This perspective strongly influenced how Chris crafted his interviews, making them arenas in which participants were invited to actively work with ideas about inclusion and exclusion. There would be no soft options or smooth impressions, including for himself as participant. He asked teachers to respond to scenarios such as:

> You're on the school advisory council. The school has enough funding to hire one extra resource teacher (who has a Master's degree in Special Education) or 2.5 Teacher Assistants. Which choice would you make, and why? You also have a say in their job assignment. . . . What would you want them to do? (Boulter, 2010, p. 82)

He played devil's advocate:

> Some would say there are plenty of curriculum materials available to plan lessons for inclusive classes, and that teachers simply need to take the necessary time to plan more effectively. What would you say to them? (p. 82)

In the follow-up interviews, he springboarded from participants' earlier statements:

> A participant stated there's a difference between the time we spend with kids in a classroom, and the "actual time we spend teaching them." The same person said, "There are a lot of things you have to do before you even get to the curriculum." What do you think they meant by that? (p. 83)

The interviews were dynamic spaces of debate and negotiation that prompted Chris to deepen his self-reflection, considering his role as leader and mediator of inclusion policy. Teachers' positions were not simple; they sometimes expressed opposing views within one interview. Fullan's (2001) comment, "If meaning is easy to come by it is less likely to be powerful" (p. 19), was frequently in Chris's mind as he worked on analyzing policy texts, interview transcripts, and his own written reflections.

Through this process, Chris was able to come to a critical, multilayered interpretation of teachers' responses to inclusion. For instance, one of this participants, "Lex," objected to "included" students describing themselves in terms of disability labels, such as "dyslexic." Listening carefully and critically to Lex, Chris wrote:

> There were complications when Lex voiced concerns over labeling students. He expressed worry that labeling kids might have detrimental effects. He told me "We're not supposed to do it, but we do." The issue became why he saw labels as detrimental, and what it might limit the child from. It did not appear that decrying labeling was a means for Lex to be more inclusive; more open to stretching the boundaries of what "normal" meant. Rather, it seemed he feared labels were presented as an excuse not to accomplish the standardized outcomes. The use of labels represented a threat to how he felt SN (special needs) students should be treated in his classroom. Labels might take him further away from the homogeneous, uniform program he desired. (Boulter, 2010, p. 122)

Keep in mind that Chris and Lex were colleagues throughout this process. This critique was not motivated by any desire to undermine educators but rather was viewed as a way to understand barriers to inclusion in ways that spoke to teachers' experiences.

As a result of his analysis, Chris came to some practical recommendations for policy and practice that, in his role as school leader, he was able to advocate. He argued in favor of more responsibility for classroom educators in developing assignments for paraprofessionals, a role that had been allocated to specialist resource teachers. There should also be greater rotation of the resource role, enabling more classroom teachers to gain insight into the diversity of learning needs within the student population. Possibly the most significant recommendation was for more honest plain-speaking about the tensions and contradictions of working toward the desirable goal of inclusive education:

> Policy makers have managed to make the struggles inherent in this contradiction a very private matter for teachers; something they are to keep to themselves, internalize, and cope with behind classroom doors. . . . My recommendation is for jurisdictions to structure teacher conversations in ways that frame contradictions as dilemmas, rather than problems that have concrete solutions. Conversations should center on negotiating a balance, rather than strictly trying to solve a problem. (p. 122)

Here, taking a practitioner inquiry approach to researching an important educational problem involves a deep, critical engagement in which insider knowledge is crucial but never taken for granted. It maintains respect for educators while keeping students' right to learn constantly at the fore.

CONCLUSION

In considering what made this project one of the "most impactful" experienced by teachers, a number of aspects is evident. First, the diversity within the group was a significant strength, particularly from the perspective of pursuing the goal of inclusive education. The group included mainstream and general educators, classroom practitioners, leaders, school-based and system-level professionals, and teachers and university researchers. This fostered respect and collegiality within the group. Critical questions and diverse perspectives were valued as collective resources; all broadened their awareness through learning about one another's contributions to inclusive education.

Thinking inclusively about schooling also challenged us to consider forms of exclusion and disadvantage that may be experienced by educators. While debates in the field have often pitted special education against inclusive education, model against model, our group included educators working in specialist and in general education contexts. We had to listen to one another and value one another's professional history, knowledge, and practice. For some practitioners, their participation in the project was an opportunity to experience professional acceptance and recognition that had been hard to find in their careers. Thus, taking up the role of inquirer provided a means to access respect and acknowledgment for their commitment to supporting the students who were often the least valued in their schools.

Exploring how to think about difference was crucial throughout this process. We were all confronted by the question of which kinds of difference counted in our contexts. Establishing difference can be a means of attracting resources. Indeed, the Targeted Populations Unit, which funded this project, had been established to manage resource allocation on the basis of difference. Some of the educators' contexts were in schools set up to cater to categories of students viewed as different from those served by the mainstream. This was the case for Dave, principal of Seekworthy, and for Ruth, teacher at Queens Park (see above). However, on reflection we found that some kinds of difference were highlighted and others were overlooked in each of our contexts, regardless of whether it was primarily a specialist or mainstream facility.

Expanding our focus to include and value all kinds of difference was a significant shift in thinking for many of the educators. Those whose learners had been categorized in terms of their disabilities began to consider the significance of other dimensions of difference, such as culture, language, and gender. This shift took place at the level of the individual student, the whole school, and beyond. For some educators, this prompted new forms of connection with the families that made up their school's community.

In practical terms, this was a well-resourced project. We were fortunate that a leading administrator was inspired to adopt an inclusive model of education as well as to embrace practitioner inquiry as a means of exploring better ways to meet the goals of inclusion. The educators were supported with funding for their studies and time to attend meetings and undertake their inquiries. Their final presentations were attended by representatives of the funding unit and there was every indication that the interest shown was genuine.

We were buoyed by the sense of joining an international community of educators and activists and contributing to a global movement of inclusive education. Studying policy documents and programs globally enabled local teachers to connect their work with this broader movement. Through reading and in some cases through direct contact, we connected with the inclusive education movement and its teacher research network. Dave, for instance, could connect his work at Seekworthy with Aboriginal education research undertaken nationally and in other parts of the world.

The Inclusive Education Project continued to have a ripple effect well beyond its 12-month duration. Our interviews showed that it provided the impetus for educators to continue their work in both inclusion and inquiry. Russell told us:

> I think it took me out of being at a site and working diligently at a site, and gave me comparisons and then expansions, and the ability to say: "What we're dealing with here has got more dimensions to it than you would see if you didn't get outside the walls."

Russell went on to conduct a study tour of North America in extension of his inquiry into the role of school services officers. This ripple effect also affected the university researchers who were privileged to work with these educators through their inquiry process. For the research leader, her learning fed directly into her supervision of doctoral students working in the field of inclusive education, located in diverse contexts that included Canada, Malaysia, and Korea. Chris's incisive study shows how this ripple of impact continued to inspire educators to investigate inclusion, motivated by their commitments to ensure that "inclusion for all" really does mean "all."

CHAPTER 6

The Boys' Literacies Project
Teachers Exploring Students' Literate Lives

The Boys' Literacies Project was nominated by some of its participants as the "most impactful" project they had been involved in. Practitioner inquiry often starts with a teacher's concern prompting a search for a new strategy. This case illustrates the importance of considering where teachers' concerns come from. The project was initiated in the context of substantial political and community pressure being brought to bear on schools to change literacy teaching approaches to produce improvements in boys' performance. In this chapter, we describe how educators were engaged in unpacking the theories of gender and learning that underpinned these arguments. In designing and implementing a collaborative practitioner inquiry project responsive to these arguments, new knowledge was produced about boys' participation and relationships, substantially impacting teachers' perceptions and practices. We describe particular interventions that teachers designed, the resources they drew upon, and the ways in which dialogic conversations deepened the whole team's analysis of issues related to boys' participation in literacy in and out of school.

TREADING CAREFULLY INTO THE FIELD:
STARTING POINTS FOR THE PROJECT

Educational research is a highly political field where there are no innocent questions—research always comes from somewhere and seeks to take the field somewhere else. Exemplary in this regard is the field of literacy education; teaching children or adults to read, write, speak, listen, and view has been fraught with debate since the inception of public schooling (Cormack, 2011). The Boys' Literacies Project traversed such a fraught landscape—indeed, the politics of literacy could be said to have provided the impetus for the research. Since the mid-1990s, there has been a growing media and political interest in the issues of boys' education. The stated reasons for this attention include persistent data showing boys lagging behind girls in many aspects of achievement in schooling, particularly literacy, and calls from some elements of the community have called for scaling back affirmative action on girls' education, especially in mathematics and science, to attend to boys' problems. Although this call for action has been heard across the globe, including in the United States (Bushweller, 1995), England (Younger & Warrington, 2005), and the Caribbean (Kutnick, 2000), it was particularly strong in the authors' context, Australia. In the early 2000s, the federal government commissioned two major research studies (Alloway, Freebody, Gilbert, & Muspratt, 2002; Lingard, Martino, Mills, & Bahr, 2002; Younger & Warrington, 2005). In June 2004, then Australian prime minister John Howard announced the allocation of $19.4 million to create better approaches to boys' education. This intensive interest in addressing boys' education in Australia was the subject of a Fulbright scholarship project whose author returned to the United States to promote a similar movement there (Weaver-Hightower, 2003).

Schools were under pressure to show that they were dealing with the issue of boys' "disadvantage" and began to develop their own programs and practices that, in turn, were reported in educational forums and the media. As a result of the high visibility of this issue, "policy entrepreneurs" (Ball, 2006, p. 21) began offering professional development courses and packages to schools featuring solutions for the "problem" of boys' education. Curriculum leaders in the school system reported receiving many requests for support from schools and teachers. In this context, one of our state's major schooling providers, the Catholic education system, initiated discussions with the authors, as literacy researchers, about how best to respond. They were concerned that some schools were taking advice with little research evidence such as the idea that painting classrooms particular colors would lead to better learning for boys. Significantly, in a system that included both coed and single-sex schools, there was a potential for contradictory messages, as some advice implied that boys' learning was suffering at the expense of support for girls.

Fortunately, the system leaders had a great deal of faith in their teachers and school leaders and wanted action on these issues to reflect and grow out of good practice in dialogue with research. The university academics were asked to establish a research project that would be driven by practitioner research, would include the system's curriculum specialists, and would produce professional development materials to be made available to all teachers and school leaders across the system. The project was funded over 2 years to provide time for four academics and two teacher researchers from each of six schools serving students in the middle years to participate, plus a part-time research assistant to provide support for the research. Three literacy support consultants from the system's curriculum team also participated in team meetings; the intention for them to carry on the work after the funding phase was completed.

The project was, from the outset, a practitioner inquiry project, but one that received its impetus from the school system, whose leaders engaged academic staff to support the process. The advantage of such external support is that it often encourages and enables work across school sites, and even across state boundaries if federal support is involved, something that is difficult for school sites to enact, let alone a few teachers at one site. Of course, there are potential downsides to such support. Traditionally, practitioner inquiry arises from practice and the questions and aspirations of practitioners, so there is the potential for sponsored projects to colonize teachers' concerns and intentions. This danger is recognized in the literature (McWilliam, 2004), and there are indeed systemic projects that require teachers to take on particular teaching approaches and "research" their effects. On the other hand, there is also no "pure" practitioner research that arises simply from a practitioner's question or concern. Questions, worries, aspirations, and so on are socially mediated. Thought of this way, all practitioner inquiry must be a negotiation between the personal and professional, the private and public, the local and global, especially if the research is to have an impact beyond the individual practitioner.

This introduction has provided a sketch of the context in which the Boys' Literacies Project was formed. That context strongly shaped the project, especially in its early stages. The project design had to take into account the contradictory and highly charged nature of the claims and counterclaims swirling around the issue of boys' education, especially boys' performance in literacy. The design incorporated three kinds of engagement by inquirers:

1. *Engaging with texts.* Here, the team encountered diverse views about boys, gender, and literacy articulated in different texts, including research articles, professional communication, policy documents, advertising, and media products.
2. *Engaging with students' perspectives.* The team investigated what literacy learning meant and how it was practiced by boys and girls, both in and out of school.
3. *Engaging with practice.* The teachers undertook two cycles of action research, responding to insights from the previous two phases to incorporate new strategies into their literacy teaching in a range of curriculum contexts.

PHASE 1—ENGAGING WITH TEXTS

Reconnaissance as a phase of practitioner inquiry involves an investigation into the issue at hand—the questions being asked, the context for the issue, the solutions offered, what has been tried before, and so on. Working with texts was an important strategy in opening up the issue for discussion. University researchers assembled a reader that was made available to all team members and included excerpts from government reports on boys' education, book chapters, and relevant journal articles (examples are included in the following discussion). One or two articles were read between meetings and discussed when the group assembled twice per term. It was noted that much of the literature assumed a problematic relationship between boys' in-school and out-of-school lives, with the latter seen as establishing masculine identities somehow antithetical to educational participation and achievement, particularly in literacy. For example, Lingard and colleagues (2002) identified boys' "cultures" as problematic, citing

> an apparent non-engagement with schooling in many boys' cultures . . . It is important to note that boys from low SES backgrounds do not have equivalent cultural capital in terms of financial and educational resources at home to support their learning outside of school. (p. 36)

Similarly, Younger and Warrington (2005) identified "laddish" cultures in boys' peer groups as a key explanation for their differential outcomes, pointing to

> the need to understand how important it is for many boys to be accepted by other boys, to enable them to identify with and act in line with peer group norms, so that they are seen as belonging . . . rather than as different. Such acceptance is often dependent on an act, negotiating an acceptable identity, and incorporating aspects of laddishness of behavior and risk-taking. (p. 18)

However, it is interesting that the research these reports were based on, with only minor exceptions, did not actually explore or engage with these so-called boys' cultures. (For a fuller discussion of these issues in the context of the project, see Nichols & Cormack, 2009.) This raised the issue of how we as a group of practitioner inquirers could stretch our attention beyond the classroom to meaningfully engage in boys' lives outside of school.

Media texts confronted teachers with some provocative teacher-blaming and school-blaming stances. For instance, one article called "It's a Bloke Thing" (Slattery, 2003) featured references to popular culture (such as the movie *Fight Club*) and was based on an interview with a school principal who blamed the "crisis" in the education of boys on the absence of "male role models." By way of explanation, the term *bloke* is an Australian colloquialism for a man, but with a bias toward a more muscular, active, and traditional view of male culture. The use of this term in the title gives the flavor of the Slattery article, which promoted a form of "re-masculinization" of schooling for boys. This raised the question of how women educators (who made up the majority of the team) could meaningfully engage in exploring and responding to the situation of boys.

A second article, entitled "The Girls Are Turning Boys into Winners" (Weidmann, 2004), reported on a school in England where boys were assigned seats next to girls in the classroom. The finding was that this practice "calms the classroom" and resulted in boys improving their academic performance. The article prompted a range of responses. Some teachers indicated that this strategy had been used informally by some teachers in their schools for many years. The discussion helped make clear the way girls may be made partially responsible for boys' behavior (something the article clearly saw as unproblematic), which led to talk about how our own research might include girls, without placing them in the service of boys.

We even looked at informal communications such as an email one member of the research team, Barbara Comber, had received from a concerned father. The email was titled "Desperation about my just turned 14-year-old son" and began by saying that both parents were "reading people"; the father described himself as a "bookworm." The parents who wrote it noted that their son was quite popular at school. However, as they explained:

> [H]e has to be pushed very hard to read anything apart from sports
> information. We have to push him to read thirty minutes a day. We are
> wondering if you can point us to any courses or make any suggestions
> to help him become more of a reading person. I can afford to pay
> for whatever is necessary. I hope you can think of something.

We noted the different values regarding literacy that were implied in the text. That the father was a self-described "bookworm" perhaps indicated that book or novel reading was the more desired literacy. His son, on the other hand, though described as not being a "reading person," did, in fact, read sports information. This raised the question of which kinds of literacy boys might value and whether these were the same as those valued in school or by parents. Discussing this email helped the practitioner research team understand that the concept of literacy, or what counts as literacy in different places, needed to be unbundled as part of the research process.

The teachers were highly engaged in discussing these representations, raising questions and debating the issues. They made connections, not just with their teaching but with their experiences as parents, and as people who had been brought up female or male. Brigitte, a primary school teacher, talked about having three sons of her own, which meant that her concerns about boys' education began from her own experience as a mother. Marissa, a high school teacher, reflected on the need to connect with her students' lives as a teacher who had responsibility for pastoral care and religious education. She saw it as a natural extension to concentrate on the boys in her classes as a group with their own interests and values:

> I think that's probably my number-one priority in my teaching, is to
> build up a good rapport with kids, and if you're going to be feeding
> them tasks that don't turn them on, I think that really does sort of, it
> pulls away at the rapport that you can have with them.

This text work enabled teachers to raise their own questions and concerns about boys and to consider these in relation to the range of positions taken in the texts we read. This process encouraged critical questioning of the various claims and problem statements. Thus, the project did not begin with setting research questions, but with asking questions about research, such as these:

1. Who/what groups are raising questions or concerns about boys and literacy in schools (and who isn't)?
2. Where are these perspectives being presented (media, events, sites)?
3. How do they represent the problem (what are their logics)?
4. What solutions are promoted or implied?
5. Is there a history to this problem (what has been said or tried before)?

Such questions have the advantage of distancing practitioners from the usual flow of thinking that may surround an issue. It helps practitioners see that an issue comes from somewhere—that is, it has authors and promoters, and even a history. The role of the media in not just "reporting" a problem, but in promoting certain perspectives on it, may emerge, as may different perspectives. Reframing the literacy debate involved an iterative process of reading, sharing, and discussion as examples of reports and newspaper articles were circulated and discussed to consider how the issue was being represented in different contexts.

The early discussion and reading had proven fruitful, even if some daunting challenges had been identified. The group understood that the issue of boys and literacy was hardly new, and that it attracted a range of sometimes passionate perspectives connected to gender and identity for boys, girls, and (female and male) teachers. Furthermore, there were claims that boys' lives beyond school were a problem for their experience of literacy within the school, for which there was little research evidence. For these reasons, the academic researchers worked alongside the teachers to codesign some data generation activities that were intended to find out more about the students in these schools and provide insights into what differences, if any, there were between boys' literacy experiences within and beyond the school.

PHASE 2—ENGAGING WITH STUDENTS' PERSPECTIVES

All schools in the project were located within a region characterized by moderate to high levels of social disadvantage, a conscious decision on the part of the school system. Therefore, the project sought to work with

Table 6.1. Inquiry Activities Engaging with Students' Perspectives

Inquiry Activity	Student Participants	Description
Survey	Boys and girls	Multiple-choice, open text, and drawn responses
Focus group discussions	Selected boys	Focused on experiences with literacy in and out of school
Home literacy audit	All students and their families	Students as co-researchers collected data using an observation schedule

teachers to better understand how boys' lives in and out of school, in such a social landscape, impacted on their literacy participation and achievement.

A feature of this phase was that inquiry activities were, to some extent, standardized across participating schools; this allowed teachers to contextualize "their" boys within a broader cohort. Though teachers would find information unique to their classrooms and schools, data collected systematically across the sites had the potential to provide more powerful insights into the questions being investigated. Some of the activities included both boys and girls, which helped the team come to grips with which aspects might be more salient to gender. The activities are summarized in Table 6.1.

Surveying the Students

The survey took a deliberately broad perspective on the aspects of students' lives that might be implicated in their experience of literacy, including new forms of literacy connected with computers, gaming, and mobile phones. The survey was designed to be easy to complete, not too long, and included some experiments in ways of gathering data (for instance, including a drawn response option). Information was requested in three broad areas:

1. What the students owned
2. The activities they enjoyed
3. Favorite place, person or possession

Nearly 100% of participants responded, unusually high for a survey. Because of the involvement of some all-boy classes, just under two-thirds of the responses came from boys. Teachers took the analysis of the survey back to their classes to give students an opportunity to discuss outcomes and interpretations. This was a useful way to double-check the validity of the results.

Particularly interesting was the absence of what teachers had predicted—namely, a clear gender difference in students' leisure activities. The survey confirmed strong engagement among the 11- to 14-year-olds with communication technologies such as the computer and mobile phone, with about three-quarters having access to both. Watching movies and television and listening to music were equally popular with boys and girls. Playing video games was more popular with boys; however, about three-quarters of girls still enjoyed the activity. When it came to hobbies/activities, two were the most popular—playing sports and reading. In both of these, there were only small differences between boys and girls—interesting given the panic about boys and reading! Only in the area of mechanics (such as car and bike maintenance) were few girls, but a significant group of boys, interested.

The invitation for the students to draw and write about a favorite possession, person, or place proved generative. Students didn't just draw things; they also showed how they valued people and places. The drawings showed that communication technologies and things connected with hobbies (musical instruments, for example) were important to many students. However, quite a few drew people, pets, and places. One response seemed to pull together all of these things. The student drew a PlayStation console, noting that it "doesn't make me bored." However, he then went on to say, "I would've done my family, but I can't draw them." For these students, home, family, pets, shared activities, and local places (for example, where sports were played) seemed to be valued just as much as technology and things. Importantly, this was true of both boys and girls.

The survey gave the inquiring educators a great deal to think about. There was a big difference between what students were telling us in their survey responses and the image of bored, nonreading, antisocial boys the press had been focusing on. New questions and research leads were developing. We noted, for instance, that computing was a ubiquitous technology in the home lives of these children and asked: How does that compare to what happens in school? We noted that sports were attended and watched by high percentages of students and asked: What kinds of texts are connected to these media and what kinds of textual practices? We noted that "playing" with mechanical things was one activity where boys had a clear preference over girls and asked: Are there implications of how boys learn to do these things for literacy pedagogy? We noted that the survey findings countered the popular assumption that boys, as a group, don't like to read and asked: What kinds of reading do boys engage in, for what purposes, and what can school curriculum and teaching learn from this?

This simple tool also showed us that research data are important for more than what can be immediately learned from them. Data were also valuable for generating educational conversations among educators and for the way the information complicated our current understandings of boys and young people. These conversations were valued by the teachers because they led to thinking about new kinds of pedagogical relationships that could be developed with the students.

Focus Groups with Boys

This activity focused on those boys teachers were most concerned about, in terms of their literacy participation and achievement. Each teacher selected a small group of "boys of concern" to take part in focus group discussions. The term *boy of concern* signaled openness about the range of ways in which boys might be causing their teachers to worry about literacy. Most teachers chose a range of different boys and not always those who were performing worst; instead, they chose some boys because of factors such as shyness, isolation, or illness. However, the most common reason given for nominating boys was lack of productivity; these boys were producing far less or poorer-quality literacy work than their teachers believed was possible. In cases where teachers did not feel comfortable singling boys out, they opened the opportunity to all the boys in their class, but they indicated to researchers who was "of concern."

University inquirers read the transcripts first and undertook basic thematic analysis before taking the information to the participating teachers for discussion and guidance regarding possible further lines of analysis. In relation to out-of-school literacies, the focus group revealed interests similar to what the survey had shown. In relation to school literacy, there were four key themes. First, the boys expressed a strong concern about the way that school *contained* (our term) them. Especially compared to their early elementary school years, the boys found that lessons were long, were conducted inside, and allowed few, if any, breaks for physical activity. School literacy activities were experienced as static in both physical and mental terms. Second, *lack of choice* was a common complaint with boys, who explained that they felt more committed when they had more say over a task's form, duration, or outcome. Third, boys mentioned a lack of *immediate relevance*. They preferred activities to be somewhat more concrete in relation to the purpose or outcome—for example, producing things for an audience other than the teacher or doing activities that were more connected to the world beyond school. Finally, *individual work* was too isolating; many boys expressed a preference for activities that allowed some social element—for example, group-work—or that allowed for movement and different seating arrangements.

Overall, the focus group discussions provided confirmation of the complexity of the issue of boys and literacy. These boys were not antiliteracy; many of them engaged in literacy activities frequently for their own purposes, especially if an expanded view of literacy was taken. However, there were issues with in-school literacies, especially involving a lack of choice and the way they enforced individual isolation and lack of variety in terms of how, where, and with whom they would be done. For the teachers, this information began to firm up hunches about what might be best to experiment with in their literacy teaching and program.

Home Literacy Snapshot

This inquiry activity involved students moving into the co-researcher role. This move was partly motivated by what we had learned in the focus group discussions about boys' desires for authentic purposes in their learning tasks. It also aimed to address a gap previously identified in the literature, and in educators' knowledge about their students, in relation to literacy practices in home and community settings. In this process, the team developed a homework assignment, which asked students to keep a diary recording their own and their family's involvement in literacy activities over the course of one weekend. This was explicitly set up as a research task for students—the form stated, "We want you to be a researcher into the literacies that take place in your household. Later, we'll use the information you collect to compare with the kinds of reading and writing that go on in the classroom to see what we can learn from that for improving what we do at school." An observation form was provided with the following headings:

- Activity (what happens, where)
- Time/day
- Who is involved
- Reading and writing involved
- Texts/resources used or referred to

The examples and prompts encouraged students (and their teachers) to adopt an inclusive definition of literacy activity—for example, "Older brother is reading the racing guide at the kitchen table. He is using a highlighter to circle horses he is interested in." Students were also invited to collect information by writing journal entries, taking notes of observations, drawing, or audiotaping. In practice, few students took up this offer, but those who did provided valuable insights.

The results of this activity indicated that a much greater diversity of reading practices was being undertaken in homes than in classrooms, though writing was less common. Altogether, 42 different reading practices were counted, with students taking the expanded view of literacy seriously by including the reading of packaging, TV captions, forms, collector cards, and many other texts. Household literacies are heavily contextualized, and this activity allowed us to imaginatively reconstruct some important activity contexts within which opportunities for literacy participation were offered. We found that four activity contexts were particularly important: sports, other leisure activities, food, and family networking. For instance, among sports-related literacy activities were reading the sports pages in newspapers, reading scores and players' names and positions in telecasts, and making written notes to facilitate the playing of ancillary games such as fantasy football.

Taken together, the three investigations into students' perspectives—the survey of their interests, the focus groups with boys of concern, and the home literacies snapshot—provided perspectives that were missing from the academic papers, newspaper articles, and government-sponsored reports we had reviewed in the first phase. Centrally, we had young people's perspectives but we also had insights from across the home and school contexts. These data contradicted reports about big differences between boys' and girls' literacy preferences and practices, but highlighted what the boys saw as concerns about school literacy activities. Armed with these insights, the team was well prepared to consider how they might move to more closely considering what went on in their own classrooms.

PHASE 3—ENGAGING WITH PRACTICE

The insights from the first two phases of the project presented some real challenges for the teachers and also confirmed some of the hunches they had brought with them to the project. The next phase involved taking up two parallel activities. First, the team worked on exploring in some detail the kinds of literacies that the students experienced at the school via a curriculum stocktaking. At the same time, the teachers began to experiment with changes to their curriculum and pedagogy based on the insights developed to this point.

The Curriculum Stocktake

Although the team had learned much about how boys' literacy learning was represented in the literature and viewed by boys themselves, we still needed to establish in detail just what literacies were being taught in class. For educators to design innovations it is important for us to appreciate our current practice; in other words, we need to know what we are intervening from. The authors had previously worked with a cluster of 10 schools to conduct detailed literacy curriculum audits, so we shared an audit instrument that had been used. The teachers undertook to record literacy learning tasks over two terms on a pro forma.

The instrument asked the teachers to note the *learning processes* involved (for example, time frame, learning activities, how students were grouped), the *texts* produced (such as essays, posters, oral presentations, maps), the *literacy resources* utilized (newspapers, text book, Internet), and the *assessment(s)* used (for example, tests, presentation, marking rubric). Along with this cover note, teachers were asked to attach copies of any documentation involved, such as handouts, assessments, and samples of students' work. Most of the teachers completed this stocktaking on three to four units of work each term, around 50 curriculum units in total. Most

(32) were from English classes, with other subjects represented, including social studies (9), science (6), and religious education (3). Units of work ranged in duration from a single lesson to several weeks.

The results of this audit showed the teachers that writing was by far the dominant mode, required for the creation of most (84%) of the *products*, while reading was involved in the *process* of most activities (84%). Together, these findings indicate that print literacy was a significant dimension of the curriculum, no matter what the subject. Over the 75 separate text products required, a wide range of text types (22) was represented, including traditional academic genres (essay, report) as well as "everyday" genres (brochure, newspaper article), and information display genres that were sometimes embedded into larger texts (map, diagram). The most popular text type was the short answer. Although teachers used a range of sources, worksheets and books were the most popular, each being used in 45% of activities. Websites were used as resources in nearly a quarter of activities (23%), slightly more than videos (18%).

Perhaps the most striking finding was in relation to the limited choice available to students. Teachers chose topics in 67% of tasks and resources in 84%. Students had some say in the timing of 12% of activities. In other dimensions of choice—modality, text type, audience, and setting—choices were hardly ever offered to students. It is fair to say that teachers were quite shocked by this outcome, which was evident across schools. They had believed their approach was more student-centered. The authors were less surprised because this had been the outcome in a previous schools collaboration.

A feature of this activity was that it began to have an impact even as it was being conducted and well before the collection was complete and the full data set analyzed. Teachers began to see patterns in their own assignments as they recorded them and began talking about the predominance of particular text types such as reports as well as the repetition of the short answer in assessments. They also noted that in contrast with the survey of students' experience beyond the classroom, traditional sources of print were dominant within the classroom. Finally, the analysis of the whole data set demonstrated the limited choice available in students' classroom literacy experiences. The teachers began to ask what might happen if more choice was offered, and what kind of choice might be productive.

Classroom-Based Action Research Cycles

In this description of the project, we have focused on the first two phases in order to demonstrate how reconnaissance, design, and analysis practices were not part of a linear process, but rather were conducted simultaneously and reciprocally. Indeed, reflection and review were deployed in each phase of the project to build on and complicate earlier assumptions about what the "problem" was and what interventions would have the best chance of making an impact.

By the time teachers had participated in considerable reading and engaged with student perspectives and curriculum analysis, they were ready to consider what they wanted to change about their literacy teaching. Teachers' initial questions reflected their concerns about boys' productivity and participation.

The project design allowed for two cycles of action research split by the beginning of a new school year, and thus, a new class (or new classes) of students for the teachers. Their first round of interventions generally focused on generating greater interest and involvement in literacy on the part of male students. They tested theories about what they believed—from their reading, discussion, and encounters with the student perspectives—would motivate and engage boys.

For instance, Brigitte asked: Will boys be more engaged in the curriculum if I make activities more connected to their interests and include more ICTs? Ben wondered: Do boys engage with texts better if the required responses are more social? Alana and Sofia (who collaborated in their inquiry) wanted to discover whether using visual texts would increase the interest of the boys in the task and allow them to show their knowledge of the topic. By the second stage, many of the teachers had shifted to a deeper and more critical engagement with issues such as identity, learning difficulties, and barriers to participation. Or they had found some aspect within an intervention that they wanted to strengthen. Ben, for example, who began by focusing on social aspects of text production in his English classes, built on that by engaging students in multimedia text production designed to explore issues of identity.

It is not possible here to provide details about all the inquiries, but we can provide a flavor of the work and the findings that emerged. What follows is based on a review of the teachers' reports, conference presentations, and reflective interviews about their research. Insights into boys and literacy were developed that were definitely a contribution to the field of professional practice and also informed our further thinking as literacy researchers. We discuss here three of the action research projects. In different ways all of them exemplified two key directions arising from the first two stages: (1) expanding the view of what counts as literacy and (2) increasing students' agency through the introduction of greater choice in classroom activities.

Brigitte: Bringing Multimodal Literacy into Social Studies. Brigitte, an upper primary school teacher, had, in the past, associated literacy learning with language arts and with the reading and writing of narrative fiction, both areas in which girls outshone boys. From the curriculum audit, she noted the untapped potential for literacy learning to occur in other curriculum areas. Brigitte also had been thinking about the relationship between her students' in- and out-of-school literacy and language experiences. She worked in a multicultural and multilingual school community, yet she realized she had created few opportunities for students to draw on their home and family funds of knowledge (Moll, 1990) to support their learning.

Brigitte was impressed with the potential of inquiry to open up new knowledge about students. She decided to give her class a small survey to discover the kinds of literacy they believed was most valuable. The boys in her class responded with a list that emphasized a wider range of texts than was encountered in a typical primary classroom, including poetry, letters, persuasive texts, research, and reports.

For Brigitte, a key was moving away from the primary school focus on literature and story, and into nonfiction work and setting up her assessment to involve writing, visuals, and talk:

> We often focus on the fiction and the writing, and this was using more research, selecting material that you want to present, using visual as well as the verbal, presenting orally, so using those skills, and I personally felt that was something that the boys really needed to work on. Although they can clown around as much as you like in the classroom, and have jokes and carry on, and they do, when they actually have to get up and present something to the class, those same kids are probably the most reluctant and the most nervous. . . . You know, to actually make them have to do that I think was a good experience for them.

She decided that the subject area of Studies of Society and Environment (SOSE) was a promising context for this kind of work. To draw on the multicultural knowledge of her students' families, she invited them to select a country to research and explicitly encouraged them to choose one for which there were out-of-school resources. Many students chose the countries of their family's origin, including Poland, Chile, Vietnam, Italy, and India.

Conventional assignments for this kind of project at that time were wall posters, written reports, and oral presentations. When the presentations of their reports were confined to poster displays and talk, the boys as a whole performed less well than the girls. The use of ICTs was still emergent in primary schools at that time, so Brigitte's decision to open up options to include digital presentation was innovative. She set up the research assignment to include a PowerPoint presentation. When the PowerPoint option was made available, the boys did much better. In fact, some of them outperformed the girls in their application of this software.

Brigitte was keen to ensure that both boys and girls assembled a rich repertoire of literacies with which to learn and present their learning. She went on to assist all students in using all their resources in different media to design and construct webpages on the Seven Wonders of the World, utilizing specialist teacher support and the assistance of knowledgeable peers to build their sites. Her project concluded with the development of a complex website incorporating all the work that her class of culturally diverse students had created over a school term in SOSE.

Though there were many signs of engagement and participation, Brigitte also wanted to see whether an objective test would support her impression of significant improvements in literacy. Indeed, each of her "boys of concern" improved his literacy when measured on the statewide ESL scales. For Brigitte, the key to success was setting up assignments in which students had a real stake and that, though they varied from business as usual, still demanded high quality from the students. The decision to bring ICTs into her classroom as a way of opening up literacy resulted in many direct challenges for her and a newly developed respect for and appreciation of the staff's technology support person. Taking an expanded view of literacy in her SOSE curriculum allowed children to engage in the curriculum in different ways and positioned them differently with respect to the display of their knowledge.

Ben: Opening to Social Learning. Ben taught an upper primary class in an all-boys school. The earlier part of the project had prompted him to reflect on his usual approach to teaching literacy. The curriculum audit and the focus group interviews with boys brought the sobering realization that he was teaching a limiting curriculum with highly individual structured tasks. He began to rethink his students' "mucking around" and reluctance to complete tasks as indicating their desire for a social space in the class. He wondered how he could draw on this social participation in the service of literacy learning.

This involved expanding his view of what constituted literacy. The key move was to understand literacy as a social practice, rather than as an individual psychological skill. Ben suspected that boys would write more if their attention was on their peers as an audience, so he developed a task that involved scripting and performing a procedure. Ordinarily, he would have taught the procedural genre through a formulaic writing task, such as a recipe. Recognizing that humor was a big part of boys' social interaction, he surprised his class by announcing that they were "allowed to be funny."

Though Ben rightly expected that the inclusion of humor would be engaging for the boys, what surprised him was its value for literacy learning. For the humor to work, boys had to really craft their scripts:

> They learned to play with language a lot more because the result was a buildup and then the punchline sort of thing, so they experienced that and that came through a lot with the lead-up work . . . they found themselves writing without really, without even trying. It was a tool.

Ben followed this activity with one that invited boys to explore their identities in an "About Me" presentation. Here, he specified the use of PowerPoint and added the restriction that there be no use of written text; the presentations had to be visual with spoken narration. Again, though, he discovered that boys used writing to develop and organize their presentations and, as he reported, some of them "got really carried away and wrote a lot of notes." For students to get carried away with writing was a new thing in Ben's class. Ordinarily, he had to demand, cajole, and constantly remind them in order to get any writing at all.

As a way of monitoring impacts, Ben also focused on a few "boys of concern" and followed their progress through the units of work.

> There were a couple of boys—for instance, W and J, who I used for focus—and they were the ones that were interviewed. I used them because I knew that they were bright but they weren't achieving their full potential. They were limited; they were often getting average sort of in the class type of thing. By the end of the year they had become what I would say are exceptional students.

When asked what had made such a difference, Ben was careful to say that the boys "growing up" could have had something to do with their improvement but that the change in the nature of assignments to make them more open and to incorporate writing more organically, also made a difference:

> I think they gained because they were more engaged and because the tasks were open. They [the tasks] were not, at the start of the year, when I limited their response.

Marissa: Troubleshooting Literacy Problems in Science. Marissa, who taught high school science, was particularly concerned that several boys in her grade 9 class rarely completed scientific experiments or produced the associated reports. Considering the major emphasis on the report genre in grade 8, she reasoned that unfamiliarity with the genre could not be the problem. The students who concerned her most were those who were hesitant to complete activities in the lab. She wondered "whether that lack of independence is due to lack of motivation because they don't understand all the things that lead up to writing a discussion, or putting all their ideas together." She decided to ask a colleague to take her lab class so she could observe the boys with the aim of discovering "the first point that they get into trouble."

As a result, she became aware that some of their difficulties arose very early in the pedagogical cycle. In fact, they appeared to have difficulty following the written instructions that were intended to support them through the sequence of tasks. Interestingly, the boys' difficulty with following the written assignment was preventing them from engaging fully with the "hands-on" components of science that boys are presumed to prefer. Marissa thought carefully about this and developed a model of the pathways of learning to account for the challenge points (see Figure 6.1).

What she had seen as a lack of independence now appeared as the boys' proactive attempts to get peer support in decoding the instructions. Marissa was already thinking about creating a more social environment in her science class. Like Ben, she was shifting toward thinking of literacy as a social practice:

> What they're talking about [the science experiment] is a group thing rather than an individual thing when they're reading. So of course a lab is a perfect place when you think about if you could remove that initial negative barrier of thinking that you have to read something as a group.

Marissa designed her intervention to address this issue. She decided to try providing instructions on audiotape as a supplementary resource to written instruction. She also grouped these boys to work together to support one another rather than splitting them into separate groups, where they had tended to be passive and reliant on their more confident peers.

Figure 6.1. Marissa's Model of the Practices of Producing a Science Report

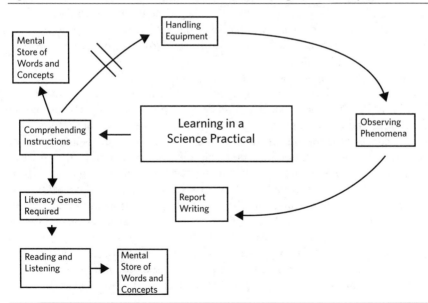

This intervention provided the boys with extra aural resources to support them through all stages of the experiment/unit and to break the cycle of dependency that prevented them from confronting and dealing with their specific literacy and learning difficulties. In the end, Marissa developed real insights, not just about boys, but about how for students with English as a second language, multiple channels of information were helpful. Her concept of literacy extended to include listening and speaking as modes for communicating knowledge. She was determined that this project would not be the end of her innovation or inquiry:

> Well, I think people have to realize that if we keep doing the same thing, that nothing is ever going to change for those children. We do have to experiment and play around a bit, and this is just the beginning. . . . [I want to] just see how do people progress through the year, once they've mastered that art of being able to listen and perform the actions of a practical.

CONCLUSION

One of the ways of understanding the impact of this project is by comparing business-as-usual to the innovations that the educators introduced into their literacy teaching. The curriculum audit had demonstrated to teachers the constrained nature of the curriculum. The home literacy audit and student surveys had shown the wider range of reading and writing practices and pedagogies in out-of-school contexts. The student interviews had underlined the disengaging effect of everyday aspects of schooling and in particular of literacy learning. The "boys of concern" from this perspective proved to be valuable informants.

One of the insights that the teacher researchers drew from the explorations in the first phase of the project into boys' experiences of literacy in the home and beyond school was that outside of school, boys and girls had a great deal more choice in what texts they used and in the ways those texts were used. Teacher observations of students and some of the students-as-researcher activities also demonstrated how fluid the roles of teacher and learner were in many nonclassroom activities involving texts—for example, a parent helping his or her child to perform a household task or to engage in a favored hobby, but the same child becoming a teacher of a sibling while playing a game. Also, out-of-school contexts involved literacy practices that were active, collaborative, and connected to achieving social objectives. This was in contrast to the lessons from the classroom stocktaking, that in-school literacy practices tended to involve little or no choice, to be more individual in nature, and to downplay or actively discourage interaction, talk, and movement.

As a result of such insights, all of the teachers, in some way, incorporated into their action research projects literacy activities that involved greater choice for the students as well as a more active and collaborative modes of work with texts. Across the projects there was also a much stronger emphasis than had been shown in the stocktaking of current practice on students having agency in relation to their work. This took different forms: It might involve greater choice about topic or text type, it might involve making decisions about with whom to work and going beyond individual work to collaborative literacy practices, or it might involve incorporating the class or others as audiences for the students' work, and even negotiating modes of assessment and rubrics for marking. This tended to lengthen the time scale of literacy activities in order to account for work beyond the classroom, time for collaborative planning, and establishing special events or forums for presenting final products. It also involved teachers incorporating the use of computers and other ICTs such as digital cameras into classroom work so that students could develop their own multimodal texts and consult the Internet to follow up on more personal questions and research.

All of the teachers incorporated elements of choice and agency in the design of the work they did with students. For these teachers, engaging boys, getting them active, and connecting the curriculum to their concerns proved to be crucial in their efforts to improve literacy. It was interesting that this element of what they did was not featured as an explicit element in any of their research questions but emerged as a strong theme in what they did—evidence of the way practitioners juggle aspects of their work, incorporating what they learn into their practice as they learn it.

This process inevitably also increased teachers' work as they juggled a range of often unfamiliar resources, locations, and (noisy) classroom interactions and events. In other words, more activity for the students meant more for the teacher—as the students' literacy practices changed, so did their teachers' work practices. One important insight from the teachers' action research was that to incorporate some of the new practices they developed in response to boys' literacy needs, long-term support would be needed and a greater range of ICT resources and technical expertise supplied within schools.

Overall, the project demonstrated the power of a joint enterprise between system and teachers, between teachers and academics, and in involving students as co-researchers. The teachers' research, combined with the other cross-project data generation, enabled the project to come up with a range of findings that could be taken up not only by the teachers themselves, but also by the curriculum consultants who worked with us to guide their subsequent work with teachers across the system. The consultants subsequently utilized not only the data generated from the project as a whole but also the various examples that had been developed by the teacher researchers, to implement systemwide professional development.

PART III

IMPACTFUL
INQUIRY PRACTICES

CHAPTER 7

Designs on Research in Practitioner Contexts

Any practitioner who has studied research in an academic setting will be familiar with the importance attached to research design. Whole disciplines are built around particular assumptions and practices to guide those who work in the field about the questions they can ask, what counts as data, and the interpretations they can deploy. An influential manual on design in educational research defines design as a series of rational choices that follow from "the philosophical assumptions the researcher brings to the enquiry" (Creswell, 2014, p. 4). The models of inquiry that result from such rational choices are described as "types of inquiry within qualitative, quantitative and mixed methods approaches that provide specific direction for procedures in a research design" (Creswell, 2014, p. 12).

RESEARCH AS A "FUMBLING ACT OF DISCOVERY"

In our experience, such rationalistic ways of conceptualizing research design have little utility for practitioners. Indeed, some argue, they have little utility for any researchers, as Hamilton (2005) notes in his critique of most handbooks produced to guide teacher research:

> [R]esearch is always a fumbling act of discovery, where researchers only know what they are doing when they have done it; and only know what they are looking for after they have found it. . . . The arguments in the *Handbook for Teacher Research* have been produced through a process of reverse engineering. The final product—a "successful research project"—is dismantled and its elements are re-assembled according to the routines of efficiency currently accepted in the handbook, cookbook or textbook genres. (p. 288, emphasis in the original)

If research is so messy, what is the point of research design? Though research is not the linear process outlined in many handbooks or manuals, it is vital to have a plan and a sense of the purpose for the proposed research that can, and should, be adapted in principled ways as the research unfolds.

It is possible for a research design to take account of the messiness of the research process and establish a map of the decisions made through the process. Having a design means that different aspects of the research can be addressed in the order that makes sense, revisited as needed and, importantly, provided with a kind of audit trail of decisions made. What makes inquiry "research" is that it is "designed." Another way of saying this is that research is *systematic* inquiry made *public*—a useful framing from Stenhouse (1975), who strongly influenced those who developed early forms of practitioner research (see, for example, Skilbeck, 1983). This distinguishes it from reflection or curiosity, which often quite appropriately remains private and ad hoc.

Practitioner contexts and practices have some special attributes that strongly affect the way research can be designed and conducted. First, practitioners are researching their own contexts and practices. They cannot, therefore, utilize traditional views of objectivity or distance to demonstrate that their own interests aren't influencing the research. Of course, there are advantages to this (discussed below), but from a research design perspective, it is very difficult for practitioners to start with theory or pure ideas, as they are always/already in the thick of the action (Schön, 1983). This means that practitioners inhabit a different kind of philosophical space from those described as the ideals of scientific inquiry. Both practically and ethically, their decisions are driven by the need to act in the here and now, and to do the best possible job they can, given their current circumstances and context (Noffke, 2008). Action and decision are simultaneous, not linear, and involve complex and recursive revision and reaction.

Practitioners use their own history of involvement in practice, their day-to-day experience of a context, and their interactions with other practitioners to guide what they do. Kemmis (2005) emphasizes the way practitioners are involved in a kind of public practice of reflexivity, learning from others, connecting with their own work, and accounting for the way the world around them changes.

Such practices of reflexivity are a resource for a crucial element of practitioner inquiry, which is *mindfulness* in the research process. At its most basic, mindfulness involves the interruption of life as usual, so that what usually goes without saying is examined, thought, and talked about. Garth Boomer (Boomer, Lester, Onore, & Cook, 1992), a champion of teacher power and leadership in curriculum in Australia, described design in this way and incorporated it into a theory of learning. For him, "Classrooms without learners with designs are classrooms where you will observe mindless training as opposed to education, which requires presence of mind" (cited in Green, 1999, p. 61). This presence of mind, for Boomer, involved learners (and he very much included teachers in this) in practices of *imagining* how to solve problems and forming *conscious* intentions to work toward solutions. He said: "'Design' embodies a classical theory of deliberate, as opposed to incidental, learning" (cited in Green, 1999, p. 61).

PRINCIPLES OF PRACTITIONER INQUIRY

On the basis of these understandings about the context of practitioner inquiry, we have defined design in practitioner research as a flexible and public process of systematic decisionmaking guided by practitioners' ethical commitments to their work and context. We have established four principles for guiding research design. These principles, based on and seeking to promote the particular strengths and aspirations of practitioner inquiry, are the following:

- Taking the practitioner standpoint
- Using multiple perspectives on practice
- Taking reflexive action
- Building trustworthy knowledge

These principles were developed out of a combination of reflecting on our own practices as both practitioner inquirers and as researchers who have utilized and facilitated practitioner inquiry over many years. We have also learned with and from many colleagues, themselves highly skilled and experienced in such work. We see these principles as a supplement to, rather than a substitute for, the useful guides to conducting action research and other forms of practitioner inquiry that are currently available. They are not offered as eternal and unchanging guides on how to design inquiries, but rather as a provisional attempt to guide design in the current context. We hope others can critique, reshape, and improve them, much in the same way they have been developed to this point, building on a rich history of work in the field. Specific design practices are described that relate to each principle with examples. Figure 7.1 provides a summary of the principles and practices outlined. The principles are designed to be applied across the work of a project and the practices can occur in different orders, or even be repeated across different phases of the research. The practices have been provided to illustrate ways in which each principle may be applied. They don't represent an exhaustive list of the possibilities. Rather, they are practices that have proven to be powerful in our context and fields of practice, implying that other practices may be needed in different times and places.

Taking the Practitioner Standpoint

At first sight, the principle that practitioner inquiry must be designed to take the standpoint of practitioners seems to be stating the obvious; however,

Figure 7.1. Principles and Practices of Research Design in Practitioner Inquiry

Taking the practitioner standpoint

- Engaging with the local
- Considering the frame
- Exploring the history of a practice

Using multiple perspectives on practice

- Reading
- Researching across sites

Taking reflexive action

- Short-term experimentation
- Cycling action and inquiry

Building trustworthy knowledge

- Refining the problem and asking a researchable question
- Deciding what are the data
- Going public

developments in professional practice fields such as education make it important to state this plainly. Reid and Green (2009) note that "mass" professions such as teaching have been under pressure from new approaches to management that have compromised the independence of professional practice and increasingly diverted responsibility for theory and research about teaching to those beyond the classroom who can produce particular kinds of (scientific) "evidence" (see also, Cormack, 2011). In contrast, practitioner research positions practitioners as "knowers" and not just "doers" who enact practices authorized by others (Cochran-Smith & Lytle, 1999). As noted in Chapter 2, inquiring practitioners tend to take practices recommended or even mandated for their sites and adapt, rework, or combine them with other practices in response to local contextual issues and learner responses. Practitioner research is designed to engage with such local and responsive practices and sees them as strengths rather than a problem of lack of "fidelity" to contextless programs.

Our own histories as practitioners have reminded us that the "caring" professions, such as teaching, nursing, and social work, arising out of women's work and practices, have a history of being carefully managed and regulated, and being relatively underresourced and lowly paid. Often, programs promoting universal "evidence-based" practices make such caring work invisible and/or lack a language to "count" it as an aspect of the work of professionals. Taking our lead from feminist researchers such as Dorothy Smith (1999, 2005), we believe that practitioner inquiry can take a stand(point) that insists that the daily experience of the practitioner counts as a significant aspect of research into professional practice. Smith shows the power of research always beginning from the standpoint of those who work within institutions, and she explores the often invisible social relations that shape what they do. The design implications of this principle impact the way decisions are made about the focus of research, the kinds of questions that are asked, and who is involved, right through to thinking about the implications of the findings.

Designing from a practitioner standpoint requires a rich view of professional practice. Programs that present "best practice" or "evidence-based practice" typically offer an impoverished view of what practice involves. They present procedures that are claimed to work universally, focusing on what we can see a practitioner do. As Kemmis (2011) says, this only ever captures "the perspective of a spectator" and not of the professional undertaking it. What a professional practitioner does is always the result of a complex array of thought, action, ethics, and history sensitive to the context in which it is enacted:

> [P]ractice seen from the inside is the most important version of practice to connect with, to engage, and to develop if we are to change the world by researching educational practice or praxis. We have tried a century of changing practice from without, on the advice of spectator researchers and the educational policy makers they advise. It has not been a century of unbridled success, in which practitioners have thrived in the light of the new knowledge research has made available to them. (Kemmis, 2011, p. 9)

Finally, standpoint is not a singular, unvaried perspective. Professionals have other lives and experiences that overlap with and enrich their work life. Issues such as gender, ethnicity, and class may play out in complex ways for different practitioners and influence how and what they research.

We have sought to honor the principle of taking the practitioner standpoint, even in the context of funded research projects built to investigate broad problems of practice. Some of the following examples arise from such projects and illustrate that projects might set out a broad field for the research, but still allow plenty of scope for practitioners to design their own complementary projects to explore issues of concern to them.

Engaging with the local. One significant way that inquiring practitioners engage in problems of significance to themselves is through direct engagement with their local context. This is often driven by the issues currently facing their students and may also arise out of challenges of connecting local concerns with broader curriculum and policy goals. For example, in a project funded by the Australian Research Council that sought to explore the links between environmental studies and literacy (Comber, Nixon, &

Reid, 2007; Cormack, Green, & Nixon, 2007; Nixon, Comber, & Cormack, 2007), a small group of elementary teacher researchers took up the challenge of connecting literacy teaching to environmental education. One teacher, Kate Charlton (2007), was newly appointed as the sole teacher in a small rural school in a community ravaged by drought and where school enrollment had dropped significantly, leading to the loss of one of the school's buildings. The school community was also facing major change in another way: A new bridge over the local river would mean the loss of an old wooden bridge with a long history:

> When the new school year started, a large patch of bare earth within the school grounds—the ghost of the missing building—was a confronting reminder of the students and teachers who were no longer there. . . . My first responsibility was to support a group of students who had suddenly found themselves without their school friends, their classroom, their familiar teacher, or even a peer group in the classroom. (Charlton, 2007, p. 68)

In designing her inquiry, Kate decided to integrate into her curriculum a unit about the historic bridge, recognizing its importance as a landmark for the community:

> Having worked all my teaching life in rural New South Wales, I appreciated the significance of this issue to the community as a whole. It connected naturally to the [curriculum] learning strand of "time and change". It seemed an excellent opportunity to link our own lives to those of people in the past. It also connected us to the many other places where small bridges had been built across tributaries of the Murray-Darling river system only to be replaced by stronger, larger, more efficient constructions. (Charlton, 2007, p. 69)

These extracts from her project report provide insights into the ways experienced practitioners weave together the givens (the curriculum, the requirements of the larger project to link literacy and the environment), the chance opportunities (changes to the local community), and local and personal ethical concerns and goals (her own long history as a rural teacher, the need to support the students through a difficult transition) when designing a research project. A further aspect of this design was the way it connected the local to the wider world, showing that local action can drive wider knowledge and skill development. Clearly, there were major challenges and risks being taken here (she called it a "daring design") when giving over large amounts of curriculum time to a shared project with a group of students working at different ages and levels:

> It would provide a focus for much of our society and the environment, language and literacy, science, art and even mathematical inquiry. We did not set out to

"save" the old bridge. Rather we aimed to experience the final months of the old . . . bridge—to consider its role, significance and meaning to our community . . . the environmental, engineering and emotional impacts of the construction of the new bridge. (Charlton, 2007, p. 69)

Perhaps the best indicator of the value of practitioner inquiry leading with a practitioner standpoint was the wider value that Kate reported gaining from the project. Although the project clearly delivered in terms of the research requirement to innovate in the area of environmental communication, there were additional and significant positive impacts on her practice and context. Her decision to use the impetus of a local community concern as the starting point also helped maintain a consistent focus on the locale and make principled decisions about the direction of the project on the fly:

My commitment to recording and continually replanning my environmental communications work within an action-research project has offered up learning about my new school, about new forms of environmental communication, and about revitalizing a small school through community action. This project enabled me to meet a wide cross-section of the community and get involved in events that had real local importance. (Charlton, 2007, p. 81)

Considering the frame. In an era when educational policy and practice are subject to close scrutiny from government, business, and the media, it is important for practitioner research to take account of how educators' work is being framed. The "frame" for educational work will include such things as the curriculum and policy texts that provide guidelines and impose requirements on practitioners, and also wider concerns such as the politics and debates that may swirl around educational topics and practices. Taking a practitioner standpoint means understanding how such texts, policies, and debates shape the experience of practice. As shown in Chapter 6, a major way we have taken up this exploration has been through reading academic research as well as media discussions and debates in order to surface positions, policies, and practices at play. In this way, we surfaced the ways that practice was connected to wider social issues and identified the aspects of the policy likely to cause controversy. The key point is that taking a practitioner perspective involves understanding how practice is represented in wider educational and social contexts. This not only helps the practitioner decide the most appropriate place to focus their research, but also helps them foresee potential problems.

Practitioners are not just professionals, and it may be that a range of their identities are tied up in the research to be conducted. In the literacies and the environment project mentioned above, early discussions surfaced strong divisions of opinions in communities in the river basin between concerns about conserving water for natural environments and the irrigation-related agriculture industries in which the teachers' communities (and even their own families) were involved. Here, teachers were not only professionals; they were also farmers' wives and members of local organizations, and they had their own commitments to the places where they lived *and* worked. As Kerkham and Comber (2007) explain:

> How teachers name and frame themselves (as greenies, farmers, activists) and the environment (in terms of making a living, issues, problems) is significant in understanding how teacher identity impacts on curriculum and pedagogical design. (p. 143)

This project demonstrated the importance of taking a generous view of the field to be researched and allowing a range of perspectives to enter into consideration. This allows for greater research openness, but also acts to protect the participants, who can shape their research to what they see as possible and/or achievable.

Considering the frame can help predict and work around challenges. For example, in early discussions in the Boys' Literacies Project, a number of teachers wanted to use multimedia, including video and films, as part of inquiries to open up what counted as literacy in their classrooms. However, others in the group pointed out the severe restrictions imposed by the school system, which meant it was difficult to use anything with a higher than G (or general) classification. Though this did lead to feedback to the system leaders in the longer term, in the short term it meant that the teachers designed projects using newer kinds of multimedia texts outside of the scope of the classification system, thus avoiding potential trouble. Early discussions in the project can help surface potential difficulties and address realistic anxieties that practitioners may have about the (possibly unintended) effects of their intentions to change their practices. We have found this especially when working with practitioners in high schools and other settings where there are high stakes for students as a result of their performance in the curriculum and assessment regimes of their school or system. In some circumstances, we have negotiated with systems or certification bodies a no-disadvantage rule for students who are involved with teachers changing their practices—a reminder that there is often good reason for the conservatism of teachers, who must consider the effects of changes on their students. For this reason, we also negotiate with practitioners an understanding that discussions about their own practice and setting remain confidential to the group, so that failures can be discussed as much as successes, and doubts and critiques find a safe place to be aired.

Burns (2007) suggests a further reason for having early consideration of how the research is framed: the need to bring out the different stories that participants may have about the matter under consideration:

In the early stages of inquiry, emergent understanding will be strongly supported if space is created for stories to be told. A story can be a brief account of something that happened, or a complex interwoven tale. If we rush to inquiry before we hear people's stories we often miss crucial understandings. Embedded in each story is a process that helps us to understand the complex interrelations between things. Stories hold an emotional content that cannot easily be accessed through official accounts. (p. 104)

For teachers, the stories are often about particular students who have troubled or surprised them. Through such stories, teachers' ethical commitments can be brought to the surface, along with the aspects of practice that most trouble them. This is a useful reminder that the frame for research is not just broader social and systemic issues, but also the personal histories and experiences that practitioners bring to the research. Creating a space to talk and reflect opens up a range of possibilities and may even "surface the undiscussables" (Burns, 2007, p. 103) that strongly shape practice. Practice in education and other professions in the current context is highly politicized, carefully monitored, and subject to frequent injunctions for improvement. This design practice involves acknowledging that practice is personal and political and not just an issue of technique or application.

Exploring the history of a practice. An important feature of what practitioners do is learning the established practices of their field or their specialization, which is largely done on the job. As an aspect of designing an inquiry into a practice or practice field, we argue that it is useful to engage with the practice traditions that have built up over time. Work on and with practice, whether it seeks to reinforce or challenge those traditions, requires some kind of engagement with its history, whether it be local and recent or over a broader range of time and/or places. Practices are never accepted as "givens," but rather are treated as constructed over time in response to certain challenges and problems: They require unpacking, questioning, and framing within the current context facing the practitioner researcher. This is not necessarily an argument for historical research, but rather a sense of history. This practice both honors the practitioner's perspective—which is, at least in part, built on tradition—and allows for it to be denaturalized and made open for review and rethinking. This design practice is an important antidote to a common tactic used by educational reformers to cast their innovation as totally new (innovations rarely are), or to dismiss something built over a long period by professionals as outdated or unscientific (Cormack, 2011). Realistically, this is something that can only be done locally and in recent times, but it also suggests that historical resources, where they are available, can be deployed. For example, in a project involving practitioner researchers inquiring into pedagogies to support students in a disadvantaged region of the city, one of the authors and a colleague (Sellar & Cormack, 2009) reviewed the work of Boomer, mentioned above, and distilled his recommendations for pedagogy from decades earlier that the practitioners found provided support for practices they valued, as well as suggesting possibilities for innovations. One of the most useful outcomes of this review of history was the way it provided a common language for talking about pedagogy between the practitioners and academics involved.

Using Multiple Perspectives on Practice

The second principle supplements the first's focus on the practitioner's standpoint by *using multiple perspectives on practice*. The concept of providing a space for communication between practitioners has informed practitioner research since action research was first described and discussed. Our experience in practitioner research suggests we expand that space of conversation to include more than practitioners in the immediate context, to take that interchange to those in different contexts and with different stakes in the field, and especially to the world of professional researchers (Kemmis, 2009). Perhaps most important, practitioner research opens space for dialogue among practitioners in the richest sense of the term. Here, we are influenced by the philosopher of language Mikhail Bakhtin (1981), who explains that the meanings we make of the world are formed in dialogue where we wrestle with what and how words mean (dialogism). Meaning is always up for grabs, and while authoritative texts/experts try to pin down some of those meanings, there are always other forces shaping new possible meanings in local and changing contexts. Bakhtin's (1990) philosophical commitment expressed the idea that people need others to better understand what they see and experience (his concept of "answerability") so that individuals understand that, though their experience and perspectives are unique to themselves, they are always limited by what they can see and experience. Individuals require others to fill out and show the perspectives they cannot possibly have on their own. Thus, practitioner research is always "public" in the sense that it is exposed to the insights, reactions, and even criticisms of others, for without such interaction a more complete understanding of practice is not possible.

Practitioner inquiry is not private reflection, but something that engages publicly with others, as informants, critics, and users of the knowledge and practices being created. As already noted, the practices of a profession arise from the history of work, sometimes involving generations of practitioners. Practice within education takes many forms and crosses contexts and locations, each of which may itself be changing rapidly. Through practitioner research, practitioners go beyond "received tradition," taking from what's available, locally and beyond, creating new conversations and possibilities as well as influencing practice. There is a community of practitioners, who range from teachers to administrators, paraprofessionals, teacher educators, publishers, and researchers, all of whom have a stake in practice and different, sometimes competing, claims on it. More than this, there are others, such as parents, students themselves, and the broader public, who have a real interest in what happens. Practitioners in one part of the field can benefit by exploring and understanding how others see and engage with their practice. Once again, this is a principle that involves some risk; for example, others might not understand a particular context, or simply may not recognize the problem that engages a practitioner. However, the benefits from engagement with other perspectives make the risk worth taking. Simply being exposed to the way others see a problem, or the practices they deploy, can be productive for the practitioner researcher. The first practice we focus on is reading, because it is through engagement with research literature that practitioners can get behind some of the key assumptions that inform their field and access key arguments that inform competing practices.

Reading. Practitioners read constantly—their environments are saturated with print in resources, on screens, newsletters, policies, and so on, but reading in and for research is a different kind of reading. Especially in academic texts, it involves encountering new kinds of language, and the extraction from practice of particular elements for examination and investigation. All of this can make some texts seem remote from the practitioners' context, but such texts are vital for helping practitioners establish some distance from their work and opening up possibilities for thinking differently about practice. This means it's important to design a research project so that there is time to identify, distribute, read, and reflect on texts about practice and the assumptions behind it—time and space to sit, read, explore, and reflect on reading is just as important as the active intervention phases of a project and may need to occur at different points as the project progresses.

Facilitators can make a real difference in this regard, especially in providing access to materials. We often found ways to register practitioners with our university library and show them how to access resources. Opportunities to share and discuss favorite papers and resources already used by practitioners are useful. Sometimes we have modeled particular kinds of research reading practices. Figure 7.2 is an extract from a list of resources we made available to the practitioners in the Boys' Literacies Project when the possibilities of engaging students as researchers in projects was raised. We didn't just list the papers, but also gave a brief breakdown of the resources made available to the researcher-reader looking for ideas on how to engage students in this way.

Making time and space for reading includes setting time aside in research group meetings to discuss the articles. It's very hard to predict how an article will be received, but even if all participants don't share enthusiasm for a piece, they can see how some have made use of it because of a

Figure 7.2. Literature Resources Provided to Practitioners

Project: A collaboration between a researcher-parent and his two teenage daughters focusing on literacies in school and at home.

Purpose: To look at how literacy functions in the lives of teenagers outside of school (e.g., for entertainment) and in school (e.g., for credentialing); to challenge teachers to give school literacy greater social purpose

Student position: The teenagers are engaged in researching their own literacies. They are credited with coauthorship of the paper. However, the writer's voice is the father/researcher's.

Technique(s): The girls kept literacy logs and then were interviewed by their father about the findings. Excerpts from these interviews are included in the article.

Data: Literacy logs documented and timed: reading (school text, novel, magazine), computer use, phone use and TV/video/video games.

Interviews asked about the functions of these activities for the participants.

Reference: Bean, T., Bean, S. & Bean, K. (1999) Intergenerational conversations and two adolescents' multiple literacies: Implications for redefining content area literacy. *Journal of Adolescent and Adult literacy, 42*(6), 438–448.

particular link to their own intentions or context. In one group discussion in the Boys' Literacies Project, teacher researchers were considering the best ways to incorporate their students' lives into their literacy teaching as a way of addressing students' alienation from the regular curriculum. One teacher drew the group's attention to a classroom incident recorded by Jones (2004) in a paper entitled "Living Poverty and Literacy Learning: Sanctioning Topics of Students' Lives." She pointed us to an observation from a class reading lesson where a student whose father was in jail (something not known by the teacher) was unable in the same way as her peers to bring *her* life into the classroom. This is the section she alerted the group to:

> Cadence sits on the floor with the rest of her classmates, preparing to listen to Ms. Lockhart's read-aloud. Her gray cotton-weave shirt is inside out and the legs of her blue jeans creep up her shins, revealing colored socks and untied, scuffed gym shoes. Ms. Lockhart begins to read aloud *Tyrone and the Swamp Gang* (Wilhelm, 1995) and the students attend closely to the story about a character considered to be a bully. The moral of the story is not to be a bully. Before the end of the book, Ms. Lockhart asks the students, "Do any of you know someone who is a bully?" The students respond with bubbling enthusiasm, mentioning names of bullies they come into contact with on the playground and in their neighborhood. Cadence raises her hand and says, "My dad is a bully." Ms. Lockhart looks at Cadence, then moves on to the next person who raises their hand. Cadence's eyes dart down to the floor and she scoots back about 6 inches. (Jones, 2004, p. 464)

For the teacher who pointed to this extract, it was an example of the dangers of bringing students' lives into the classroom. A spirited discussion among the project teachers followed in which these dangers were acknowledged, but others pointed to this as an example of how some children never feel that the curriculum speaks to their lives and the difficult topics that are unspeakable in the classroom. As the discussion petered out into a thoughtful silence, it was clear there was no single "lesson" being taken from the paper, but that it had caused people to think again about the topics that get talked about. This paper was referred to a number of times during the project by the teachers. It influenced a number of teachers to design ways for all students to share aspects of their lives in the classroom.

Researching across sites. One of the benefits of designing projects that access multiple perspectives is that it enables practitioner researchers to learn from one another. This can occur even within one site, as different roles and settings can lead to different perspectives on the same problem. Opportunities for learning increase if practitioners working in different sites and even different school systems can work together. An example of this occurred in a project on senior secondary assessment, where the project began with an extended reconnaissance involving a review of the history of support for students with literacy and numeracy difficulties in each of 10 school sites. We were able to aggregate the data collected and consider some of the patterns across sites. The strategies for identification and support reported by the schools were placed into six categories:

1. Identification (e.g., review of marks, literacy testing)
2. Individual support (e.g., withdrawal programs, use of paraprofessional support)
3. Special programs and nontraditional subject courses (e.g., establishing a homework support center)
4. Curriculum/pedagogical initiatives within courses (e.g., "mapping" literacy requirements of a course)
5. Structural and resourcing (e.g., establishing a leadership position with a focus on literacy)
6. Training and development and/or professional development (e.g., sending staff on courses)

The 10 schools involved reported 159 separate strategies fairly evenly spread across these categories. When looking across the strategies, it was striking how few were common across all schools. Only three were used by at least half the schools (literacy testing for identification, one-to-one support tutoring for students with difficulties, and mapping of literacy across subjects), while 64 were unique to one school. Discussion of the strategies by the teachers showed that although there was some confidence that the identification strategies were doing their job, teachers found it difficult to translate identification of students with problems into effective means of helping those students; there was a problem with knowing how to help *this* student as he or she worked and encountered difficulties. Also, knowing which students were experiencing difficulty and having strategies to support them could only go so far if the students wouldn't actually engage with the classroom program and attend classes—the classroom work needed to get them engaged, and maintain their commitment to improving their literacy. This proved to be a crucial starting point for most of the teacher researcher teams in deciding how they would focus their research. Most teams, in their own context, took up a curriculum and pedagogic focus in their research, attempting to design students' study in units of work that would engage students and provide flexible opportunities to help them solve literacy problems at a point of need. For example, one team decided:

> Selected focus students attend a weekly "literacy workshop" for one
> lesson per week for 14 weeks. The literacy workshop follows students'
> work experience placements and involved helping them to develop
> a digital presentation about themselves using PhotoStory software.
> This provided many opportunities for writing for which students were
> provided support at point of need.

Another school decided to trial a new Personal Learning Plan course using a "life coaching" approach, asking students to document and present their plan in a multimedia format. Another school decided to try to combine work in this same course through a focus on health and work in English class—a kind of middle school approach to building work units across projects. What many of the plans had in common was the use of nontraditional media as a way of engaging students—another school asked students to video their work placements and to use these as a basis for considering the kinds of literacy demands in that workplace. Also, by setting up special groups or lines in the timetable and teaming teachers, more flexible time was provided so that teachers could work more closely with individuals and groups of students. Each of these experiments built on insights developed out of the research design that enabled the comparison of practices across schools and the identification of the key challenges facing the schools to support students at risk in literacy.

Taking Reflexive Action

A third principle is that practitioner research provides *opportunities for reflexive action, building on experience and responding to what happens.* This principle recognizes the particular complexity of professional practice and the need for thought and action to be virtually simultaneous. It is, therefore, very difficult, in the ordinary life of a practitioner, to gain sufficient distance from practice to think about it at length and consider different perspectives. Key concepts here are those of *time* and *distance*. Time is a precious resource in professional practice contexts, but in our experience, reflection and the space for systematically thinking about that context requires "timeout." Just as a coach may call timeout so that players stop playing in order to think about how they might play better, practitioner research involves stopping the practice in order to make it amenable to reflection through which the practitioner can, in Boomer's (cited in Green, 1999) terms, develop designs for that practice. This involves time for thinking *back* (often collaboratively) on practice as well as thinking *forward* into the possibilities for change and new action. Practitioners can most effectively make such time available with the support of educational leaders who provide resources and structure workplaces that enable collaborative reflection and action. Historically, in our own context in Australia, school systems have supported practitioner inquiry where it has been built into funded research projects because the insights from practitioners have been valued, especially when considering how to address longstanding educational issues such as the performance of students who live in poverty or the connections between gender and learning outcomes. In such projects, a small number of teacher relief days are provided to allow teachers to meet away from school and to work with colleagues from other sites and regions. Equally successful projects can occur when such funding is not available, where sites structure work practices that allow practitioners the space and time to meet, think, and plan.

The concept of *distance* relates to, and builds on, the availability of time. Here, we refer to the necessary distance that the practitioner needs to establish from practice as something that flows minute to minute, where much is, of necessity, "practiced" in the sense of being able to be done without too much conscious thought and where much of what happens is taken for granted. This is not a situation to be concerned about, for if everything needed thinking out and was being met for the first time, not much would get done! However, it is a state that needs to be interrupted if practice is to be thought about, (re)considered, and (re)worked on. Therefore, the collection of research data is an invaluable and fundamental part of the design process. To collect data about practice involves a range of processes—each of which distances that practice from its everyday operation. First, decisions must be made about what aspect of the practice is to be made a focus (it's very difficult to capture everything that happens in a classroom event, so the most salient aspects need to be identified). Second, those aspects that are the focus need to be recorded in some form so that they can be examined later and perhaps compared with data from other instances of the event, or the event in a different place or time. In this way, the practice becomes a text in the sense that a "text" is any representation (writing, video, oral recording, numbers, and so forth) of an event via the aspects of it that are recorded. Practitioner research is always textually mediated because the data being considered are in some kind of textual form capturing some element(s) of practice only. This is one of the tensions inherent in practitioner research. Although it focuses on practice, it necessarily interrupts that practice and turns it into text, which is only ever a partial representation of the complexity that is practice. However, there is power in text, as Smith (1990) makes clear, for it is through texts that people's lives are regulated, and practice is often shaped in ways that are invisible to the users. Texts define and denote the ideas and actions that are considered relevant or significant; therefore, it is vital that practitioners learn to "read" the texts that shape their practices and create their own texts that can enter into dialogue with those ideas. Strategies for creating, using, and reading texts are considered in Chapter 8 on analysis.

Through the use of both time and space, practitioner inquiry allows for collaborative learning, analysis, and reflection. Because of its collaborative nature, such research can never be pinned down from the start, so the design needs to account for revisiting goals, assumptions, and strategies as the research progresses.

Short-term experimentation. One way of identifying aspects of practice on which to work is to build in a phase of short-term experimentation with ideas, especially for how to generate useful data about practice. An example of this involves a project by an individual practitioner working in the early-years setting of a Child and Parent Centre (CPC—a site combining elements of preschools and kindergartens). However, while the practitioner was researching individually, her study was also undertaken as part of a graduate certificate program for experienced practitioners, where courses were designed to support the development of skills and knowledge in practitioner research. A significant innovation in this course was that practitioners were encouraged to think and read about data analysis before they finalized the focus of their research, so the design here meant that data generation and analysis *preceded* finalization of the research focus. The example illustrates reflexivity in action, where the opportunity to generate and think about data positively influenced the design of the project.

For Clarice, the teacher involved in this project, the initial impetus for her research was a concern about the quality of young children's involvement in activities that were designed to promote social and educational development. In a CPC serving many Indigenous children, she noted big differences in the dynamics of group activities depending on who was involved. Some of the children's behavior puzzled her. She began by focusing on one student:

> I began, with the very best of intentions, to make observational notes of my focus child during activities. I found that I could only make

notes for a very short period of time and not very concisely, being the only adult in the CPC created a predicament. How could I effectively collect some data?

She tried sound-recording group activities involving the child, but although having a microphone placed inconspicuously on tables seemed not to affect the children, the quality of the recording meant that it was difficult to hear some voices and distinguish among those talking. However, this was enough for her to realize that it was the group dynamics, rather than one child's involvement, that were of the most interest. She made this realization when the arrival of two quite troubled boys to the center seemed to dramatically alter the ways children participated in activities. After experimenting with a hand-held camera, which caused distractions and had limited memory, she invested in a new-generation micro-size camera with greater storage that could be put on a tripod and set relatively inconspicuously in a corner. This strategy produced good-quality recordings, and it was relatively easy to work out who was doing and saying what. At this stage, a workshop conducted on data analysis as part of her study course proved crucial to the project's direction because Clarice was introduced to the use of written transcripts as a way of displaying and analyzing data on talk. She tried making a transcript of a group session from one of her recordings, using headphones and the ability to rewind and pause the recording in the process, and found that the transcripts opened up new (and sometimes uncomfortable) insights into what was happening in her CPC:

> Stripped bare of body language, sights, and sounds, the transcript provided me with a radically different view to what I previously held of the language these children used. I was unprepared for what I discovered and, admittedly, I was surprised and disappointed by parts of it. I became astutely aware of the extent that the context of children's language has on shaping my impressions of their "talk." Carrying out this activity has provided me with the valuable opportunity to disengage from the context and concentrate purely on the "talk" that took place. More transcripts will need to be done to verify that this excerpt is the norm. There are many tangents that could come from this data. . . .

For Clarice, who had done a lot of work with the children on cooperative and inclusive play, the transcripts showed that there was a lot going on in the activities of which she was unaware, and that her assumptions about what was happening led her to see/hear only a fraction of what occurred. As a result, she was able to clarify what she wanted to explore in her own inquiry using one key question with two subquestions:

What does social interaction look and sound like in our CPC?
- What cooperative language is used?
- How inclusive is the language?

Here, her reading of research also helped her as she identified some frameworks that could be used in analyzing her transcripts, which involved incorporating analysis of types of play she observed using a social play continuum with concepts of social learning drawing on the work of Vygotsky (Light & Littleton, 1999).

Cycling action and inquiry. Although this is a common design practice in practitioner inquiries, we have found it useful to consider the different ways in which inquiry and action might interact within a project that utilizes the action research spiral (Kemmis, McTaggart, & Nixon, 2014). Figure 7.3 shows a guide used by the first author when introducing the concepts in the Inclusive Literacies Project described in Chapter 5.

The key is that inquiry and action can occur in any order, but the order designed into a project can make a difference. This is an example of the way that the design of practitioner inquiry projects allows for flexibility and the flow of action and inquiry. The example of Clarice inquiring into approaches to gathering data in the previous subsection on short-term experimentation is a good example of this flexibility.

Figure 7.3. Relations Between Action and Inquiry

Action and Inquiry
- ❏ When I want to change something, I act
- ❏ When I want to find out something, I inquire

Inquiry *Before* Action
- ❏ When I am not sure what action would be best
- ❏ When I am not sure what others have tried before me
- ❏ When I need to know how those who may be involved feel about this action

Inquiry *During* Action
- ❏ When I want to understand how a process is unfolding
- ❏ When I want to see how the action is impacting those involved

Inquiry *After* Action
- ❏ When I want to find out the consequences of an action for those who were involved
- ❏ When I want to understand why things occurred in the way they did

Building Trustworthy Knowledge

Our fourth principle is that practitioner research seeks *to build knowledge that practitioners find trustworthy and has use value for the profession.* As has already been discussed, practitioner research requires engagement with the broad profession, seeking to make a positive contribution to practice, but to do this, those who may use the results need more than just access to the research; they also need to find that the research speaks to their own situation and to be reassured that the research is trustworthy. Practitioner researchers will have encountered the technical concept of "validity" if they've undertaken courses on research. This concept requires that the research actually address the phenomenon it is exploring in such a way that the findings can adequately draw conclusions about it. Different kinds of validity ("face," "construct," and so on) are used in professional research as technical design issues and are most relevant to larger-scale studies concerned with sampling or making predictions about effects on populations. It is a concept that isn't particularly useful to practitioner researchers whose research is strongly connected to their contexts because they aren't abstracting/extracting phenomena from their daily instantiation. Also, practitioners will be the primary users of the research outcomes, so they understand how the phenomena being studied work in real life. However, if practitioner research is to move beyond a minor role in the development of the profession, it needs to be of use to more than the practitioner her/himself and speak to others in the field, including policymakers and professional researchers.

Practitioner research has a head start in this regard: It is embedded within the work life of practitioners and, therefore, avoids many of the difficulties of access to practice that can face large-scale projects. Importantly, practitioner research can provide access to the context within which practices are deployed (for example, the reading lesson, the selection of courses by students), potentially better explaining why, how, and when certain practices work (or do not). This is what research conducted by nonpractitioners often ignores. Like Reid and Green (2009), we argue that "there is value in giving attention to mundane, naturalistic aspects and dimensions of professional life and work, rather than to isolating and decontextualizing particular features, episodes, and operations, as in various conventional forms of scientific research" (p. 169). This is to argue that including the everyday experience of practitioners has the potential to improve the use value of research more broadly, and specifically to make it speak to those who must implement policies and improve their practice. From a design perspective, this means research needs to be attentive to the mundane matters that often go without saying in daily work life. It could be that the nature of the room, the furniture and its layout, or the angle of the sun through the window are worth considering. Photographs, journals, accident and repair forms, and supply lists could supply equally useful information. This connects with our first principle of researching from the standpoint of the practitioner in that practitioner research starts with and returns to the actual, embodied practitioner and shows not only how the she/he acts, but also how she/he is acted upon and enmeshed in social, physical, architectural, and textual practices.

The embedded advantage of practitioner research—its situatedness in the lives of practitioners—is also a source of potential criticism, for such research can be regarded as being affected by the interests of the researcher. How can others know that the research being conducted by insiders is not simply reproducing their prejudices but rather is providing trustworthy insights into the problem being researched? It is important that practitioner research engage with issues of fairness and transparency, and acknowledge its limitations, while also staking a claim for the significance of insider research. A key concept in this regard is that of "trustworthiness," whereby practitioner research establishes that the data it uses provide useful insights into the problem being researched, and that the conclusions drawn from analysis are reasonable and have implications for others. Fish (2009) compares the role of a practitioner researcher to that of a hero in a picaresque novel such as *Don Quixote* who encounters challenges and risks on the journey and does not know the eventual worth of his or her efforts until its conclusion. For the reader, it is only worth sticking with such a story when "there is a firm belief in the integrity of the story and its narrator (as is also the case in a research report)" (Fish, 2009, p. 142). Thus, practitioner research, if it is to be seen as trustworthy or to have "integrity," must tell its story in a way that engages the reader and shows how challenges were met and what lessons were drawn from them. Going public—whether through writing, telling, showing, or a combination of all three—is vital along the way *and* at the conclusion of a project, for it is not until the conclusion of a journey that its full meaning can be understood:

> In both research and the picaresque, then, the development of understanding of both the hero and the reader depends upon recognizing, capturing and interpreting a range of complex events, whose details are never fully revealed and whose meaning changes with each changing direction of the journey. Understanding is achieved by unraveling a range of possible interpretations of each happening *and* of the overall journey. (Fish, 2009, p. 142, emphasis in the original)

Refining the problem and asking a researchable question. For practitioners taking up a researcher stance, one of the key challenges is asking a researchable question. Using questions posed in academic research is usually outside the scope of a practitioner project and, often, not the kind of question that engages with the particular challenges faced in the practitioner's context. Armstrong and Moore (2004), in their discussion of the role of university researchers supporting practitioner researchers, argue that the problem is designing a question that is both researchable and "actionable." They note that university researchers could "transform a broad question or area of interest into a researchable question"; however, practitioners had a stronger sense of "what would make a question actionable" (Armstrong & Moore, 2004, p. 22). Therefore, they believe that forging this connection requires dialogue between university and teacher researchers. This is a useful formulation because it means that the question needs not only to be answerable within the context of the proposed project, but must also help lead to action in the practice context.

The questions and comments in Figure 7.4 are a resource we used with colleague Hilary Janks when working with educators to design a research project. Some had expressed an interest in exploring popular culture and its impact on their students, so this was developed as a discussion starter for the process of coming up with a research question. The goal was to show that questions can close down or open up a topic. They can also suggest

Figure 7.4. Versions of a Question and Their Inquiry Potentials

Question	Inquiry Potential
Can I help my students understand the dangers of "skinny" images in advertisements?	Closed and assumes a problem–solution relationship
What responses do my students have to the presentation of "skinny" images in advertisements?	Opens up the subject to a range of possible responses
What body images are presented in advertisements?	Broadens the topic (from "skinny" to "body image") and opens to a range of possible images
What body images are presented in advertisements and how do they impact my students?	Includes consideration of effects
What patterns are evident in the relationship between images of bodies and types of advertisement?	Suggests a possible avenue of analysis
What advertisements featuring body images do my students find most appealing and why?	Opens to questions of desire rather than seeing the images solely as a danger
What body images are presented in advertisements in my students' four most popular magazines?	Scopes the inquiry by identifying a manageable data set
Who gains from the ways that bodies are represented in the advertisements? Who is disadvantaged?	Considers effects and the fairness of those effects

avenues for data generation and introduce ethical considerations, such as considering who gains or is disadvantaged by certain practices.

Deciding what are the data. Manuals and guides for inquiry provide useful overviews of the kinds of data that might be generated within a project, and the teachers we have worked with have found them useful. However, we have found that they tend to focus more on what might be called "purposeful research activities," which are produced for the specific purpose of the research at hand. Although these are important, we found that practitioners may ignore a great deal of information that is available on hand. Figure 7.5 shows a chart produced by the first author where she modeled the kind of data she considers when conducting research as an academic practitioner.

As the chart shows, possible data for research on teaching include material generated during practice as usual. Materials become data when they are considered for analysis in relation to research questions. So, for example, when Alana and Sofia (see Chapter 6) trialed the use of visual texts within their studies of society and the environment lessons, they realized that they could use the students' responses to these texts—spoken and written—as data to determine how much students knew about their local area when that became a focus for their work. When the teachers in the Boys' Literacies Project conducted the audit of their literacy lessons, as described in Chapter 6, they were able to see the patterns of choice, mode, and topic that dominated their curriculum. This practice is discussed in detail in Chapter 8 on analysis. The key insight from the perspective of analysis is that materials become data when they can provide material for analysis in relation to the research questions.

Figure 7.5. Generating Data for Research on Teaching

Data in the school office/on the system

- Demographic information
- Student records

Data in my filing cabinet/computer

- Lesson plans
- My student records
- Previous students' work

Data collected in the course of teaching/learning

- Observations
- Classroom seating plans and movement charts

Going public. The final practice for enacting the principle of building trustworthy knowledge is going public with the insights developed from practitioner inquiry. Going public means going beyond the private reflection that all teachers deploy, and even discussion among close colleagues, to share with others the insights developed from inquiry and the means used to develop them. By "going public," we mean that the practitioner provides an account of his or her research that is designed to explain to those not immediately involved what was done, why, and what was learned. Usually the public audience is other practitioners, or members of local educational communities, but it can be much wider and involve presenting to practitioners from other schools, systems, and places, or even publication and presentation in academic form, such as conferences and journals. We argue that the benefits of going public arise not only from the act of presenting or publishing, but also from the process that leads up to it, and what might follow from it. Thought of this way, going public is a practice that is part of the research process, and not something that happens after a project is complete.

In the lead-up to a presentation or publication, a major benefit is the impetus to write about, and consequently work out, what has been learned from the research project. The processes of writing, refining, and understanding are integral to working out what is worth saying about the research. In designing academic programs involving practitioner inquiry, the assessment often provides a basic form of publication. However, we usually build into such courses the opportunity for practitioners to present the results of their work to their peers or even wider groups. Similarly, when designing collaborative research projects, opportunities for presentation and/or publication are built in from the start. Both the Boys' Literacies Project (see Chapter 6) and the Literacies and the Environment project already mentioned in this chapter included conferences at which practitioners presented their findings. In the case of the Boys' Literacies Project, this also involved presentations to teachers and leaders from across the school system and, for some volunteers later, presentation at a national literacy conference. In the Literacies and the Environment project, in addition to a project conference, a group of volunteer teachers worked with academic partners to develop chapters in a published book (Comber et al., 2007).

In our experience, writing for presentation or publication is a difficult process for any researcher, and practitioner researchers are no exception, especially because this kind of writing involves a set of skills not usually utilized in day-to-day practice; therefore, it is a process that requires time and collegial support. Making time in the design of a project for trial presentations or the sharing of draft findings can help, as can workshopping draft texts. However, it is the deadline for the presentation or the production of the text that is fundamental for concentrating the thinking and producing the text. Ben, who was associated with the Boys' Literacies Project, was able to explain how the demands of presenting and publishing helped him develop a range of skills. For example, the process of preparing his presentation was significant in helping him crystallize what he had learned about boys and literacies:

> I guess it was, because we had to do some presentations, getting your head around what you'd actually done and digested it, and pulled it apart, and then sort of formalized it. It just allowed me as a teacher to understand exactly the kind of learning that I've done so I could discuss it.

A further benefit from conducting presentations and sharing findings is the skills the educators develop for communicating about curriculum and pedagogy to other educators (discussed in Chapter 4 on the impacts of practitioner inquiry on career). Educators could find the right words to explain themselves to their colleagues; they could express themselves in terms that connected with practitioners' concerns.

The related benefit from the conceptual work required for summarizing findings and presenting them is that practitioners broaden the conceptual and linguistic resources they have to communicate about their work. For example, through both formal and informal presentations, Ben honed and expanded the language he could speak and was able to translate his work into new contexts. He also learned that what might work in one context did not necessarily work in another. As he said about one of his presentations, where he found that teachers weren't interested in the implications for thinking about literacy as a concept after a successful description of the multimedia work he had done:

> I think it was a bit too academic, to be quite honest, so I think a lot of the teachers have an understanding, but the big words they don't get!! So yeah, I think basically that was too academic for them; they weren't interested.

He explains that after presenting the final outcomes of his work with his staff, he was able to work further on the data he had generated, combine those data with other materials, and turn all of it into an application for a major award, showing that he could translate the implications of his research into different contexts, from his own school to a national curriculum forum. Overall, those who were most enthusiastic about the process of going public were those who were able to build their skills in this area and translate them into other aspects of their work.

It is worth noting that Ben also experienced some challenges in the process. He found himself being "grilled" about his work at a conference. His advice to others was to "make sure they're supported in the presentations."

This is a reminder of another benefit (and challenge) of going public: It provides a forum for the research processes and outcomes to be validated or challenged, leading to further refinement and thinking. The challenge lies in supporting practitioners to engage in forums where alternative or supporting explanations and experiences are made available. Though this is a new skill for many practitioners, it is a necessary one if practitioner inquiry is to make a contribution to the wider research enterprise as well as to other practitioners. The reports from educators involved in the IPI project and interviews showed that involvement in practitioner inquiry projects helped develop these skills, even if they were hard-won.

CONCLUSION

This chapter has presented four principles as guides to the design of practitioner inquiry projects and has illustrated a nonexhaustive range of practices that embody those principles in action. We have deliberately highlighted some practices not featured strongly in traditional guides to research design so that this work builds on decades of work in practitioner inquiry and supplements those guides.

Inquiries that are based on these principles and deploy such practices may look, at first sight, very different from one another, because the principles require a flexibility of practice that allows research to account for and learn from professional work contexts. Practitioners come to inquiry for different reasons: some to experiment with a practice they have a hunch about, others with a wish to understand the thinking behind practices, and others to challenge usual practices because of a concern about the way they affect particular students. Acting, reflecting, or reading can each be a legitimate starting point for a research process, which may well feel like a "fumbling act of discovery" (Hamilton, 2005, p. 288). We have argued that this flexibility requires design to be guided by a set of principles that respect and utilize the practitioner's standpoint and allow it to be extended, analyzed, and critiqued. The involvement of practitioners in research is no guarantee of useful research. We have argued for a practitioner standpoint that is ethically based, tested through reflexive action, exposed to multiple perspectives, and establishes some kind of audit trail of decisions and actions, so that when it comes time to go public, the logic of the research underpins the trustworthiness of its findings. In the next chapter, we go into detail about a key aspect of this process: how practitioner researchers analyze the data they generate through inquiry.

CHAPTER 8

Analysis in Practitioner Inquiry as a Process of Encounter

Analysis is an interpretive process of active meaning-making; interpretations are not pregiven, but are produced by human practices of thinking, articulating, mediating, and reconfiguring. Data cannot speak unaided. They have to be brought into conversation with ideas and perspectives. This is a time-consuming process, requiring lingering with the data. Analysis has been described as a process of "withdraw[ing] from the stream of events" and questioning those events through the medium of the data (Altrichter, Posch, & Somekh, 1993, p. 121).

We have observed that analysis in practitioner inquiry is most generative when it is enabled through three kinds of encounters:

- Encounters with data
- Encounters with concepts or ideas
- Encounters with others' perspectives

Through these three kinds of encounters, a layering process happens. Meanings emerge and are contended with, contributing to a fuller understanding of the educational problem or issue under investigation.

There are many guides to practitioner inquiry; however, generic descriptions of methods do not always serve to open the black box of the analysis process. This chapter is not a how-to guide. Rather, in order to shed light on how knowledge is generated through analysis in practice, this chapter will provide descriptions of specific strategies as they have been experienced by effective practitioner inquirers. As facilitators of inquiry, the authors also reflect on our own roles as dialogic partners with practitioner researchers engaged in analysis.

ENCOUNTERS WITH DATA: MAKING AN IMPRESSION

Data make their own demands on the analyst. When a practitioner has determined to produce documentations of practice and treat these as data, he or she then is faced with a new set of "stuff." This stuff may be familiar when looked at in the context of everyday practice, but it assumes a different look and feel when taken out of the flow of learning events. Conversations between students, for instance, happen all the time in classrooms. Teachers catch snippets of these as they walk around the room and make on-the-spot decisions about whether and how to intervene. But when a teacher decides to place a microphone on a table and transcribe every word that a group of students say to one another, the conversation then takes on an entirely new quality. When this transcribed conversation becomes a text that can be read in the quiet time after the class has gone home, there is no longer the immediate imperative on the teacher to act. Instead, the practitioner inquirer faces a new imperative—to dwell on and notice the whole of what has now become available.

The reference to "making an impression" refers to the *data* making an impression on the *inquirer* as much as the other way round. Wenger's (1998) work on the negotiation of meaning is helpful here. He writes that to negotiate meaning, we must act in "a world of both resistance and malleability" and accept "the mutual ability to affect and to be affected" (p. 53). Inquiry data are taken from the world of professional practice. They document that world and are part of it. To state that data have "resistance and malleability" means that the data must be accorded the status of the real, yet they are also open to interpretation. This creates what Wenger (1998) calls a "give-and-take" in the meaning-making process. Data give something to the inquirer, and vice versa.

To consider this further, let us look at two pieces of data collected by teacher researchers. Each of these is an artifact of school life that would, outside of an inquiry context, possibly have little weight. The data are the kind of fragments of process that have to be consciously extracted from the flow of events. Analysis requires practitioners to contend with these pieces of the world and see what they have to give to a process of meaning-making aimed at generating answers to an inquiry question.

Weighing Brian's Words

These data take the form of an excerpt of a recorded and transcribed conversation between a teacher, Demi, and one of her grade 7 students. Demi taught in a rural school that had moved to a new system of assessment in mathematics that was focused on skills rather than assignments. Students were given a detailed Math Mastery Skills (MMS) list at the beginning of the term and were told that whenever they believed they had mastered a skill, they should plan a meeting with the teacher or a teaching assistant. Having given evidence of meeting the skill, that skill would then be ticked off on the MMS sheet.

Demi wanted to get a clearer sense of how the MMS process was work-ing and particularly whether it was encouraging students to take responsi-bility for their own learning in mathematics. She decided to record some of these meetings and treat the transcriptions as data, together with her observation notes and the MMS sheets. Among her set of transcripts was this exchange between herself and a student she referred to as Brian.

> *Demi:* Brian, can you bring your math book and your Mastery Skills checklist out to me, please?
>
> *Brian:* I haven't got it.
>
> *Demi:* Check your tray and the math book box.
>
> *Brian:* It's not there.
>
> *Demi:* Just check.
>
> *Brian:* This is dumb.
>
> *Demi:* Brian, I am meeting with you to discuss how you think you are doing and also to find out how you think we could assess your work better because at the end of the day, we need to report to your parents.
>
> *Brian:* Well, you could just watch me when I'm working and ask the others what I know.

Were this exchange to happen as part of the normal flow of events in the classroom, Brian's refusal to present his math book would probably be given little thought by the teacher. This was a usual response by this particu-lar student. The teacher's usual reaction is also displayed here—successfully meeting Brian's bluff about not having his math book.

However, when this interaction is treated as a piece of data, Brian's words are accorded a different significance. They demand to be weighed. When Demi read through this transcript, she was particularly struck by the statement, "Well, you could just watch me when I'm working and ask the others what I know." As an inquirer, Demi did not dismiss these words; she allowed them to make an impression on her. Thinking about Brian's statement in relation to her inquiry question, she saw it is offering a pos-sible alternative to the MMS meeting practice and one that merited further attention. It also raised a question: Why would a student like Brian prefer to be observed and have his friends interviewed about his work rather than meet with the teacher?

By allowing this student's words to have weight, Demi began to think differently about the nature of responsibility as it was performed in the MMS meetings. She could see that though many of her students were com-fortable with being made individually accountable, one-on-one with a teacher, others may experience this as discomforting rather than motivating. She also recognized that Brian, in suggesting that he be observed at work, was offering to be made accountable in a different way.

Attending to Administrative Artifacts

Some of the inquiring educators who have worked with us are administrators. When considering how administrative settings might function as inquiry zones, we need to look at the kinds of artifacts that educational administration produces. There are also issues of gaining approval to treat these artifacts as data. In one example, a head-office working group was developing a set of principles for the design of new preschools and schools. These principles were intended to embed concepts of 21st-century learning into the architectural and material qualities of school spaces. A coordinator was appointed to consult with representatives from across the school sector to develop these principles.

As this was a new initiative, the coordinator was interested not only in the product the group was tasked to produce (the principles), but also the process through which a democratic representative group could achieve this aim. This interest in process, and not just product, prompted her to seek permission to collect minutes of their meetings together with drafts of the statement of principles and email correspondence related to the process.

The inquiry group reportedly had an overwhelming amount of material to work with. This feeling of being overwhelmed by data is a common experience for practitioner inquirers (and for educational researchers in general). It is part of allowing data to make an impression. When the process under investigation is extended and complex, then the sheer quantity of stuff that has been collected is a striking reminder of the complexity that inquirers are trying to understand.

In this instance, the group decided to review the minutes and email correspondence and extract all suggestions made for changing the document. These suggestions were then organized according to the section of the document and the version, from first to final. Comparing the first and final versions with the suggested changes, the group then counted all changes that had been implemented. For example, they found that there were 26 changes made to a single section of the statement that concerned the way in which spaces in a school should be connected in order to facilitate 21st-century learning. Drilling down further, the administrator compared the wording of versions of a single subsection and found that between version one and the final version, there had been a significant expansion and the content now reflected a stronger and more practical alignment with the concept of 21st-century learning.

Policymaking by committee is a common function of education bureaucracies. This process is rarely put under the spotlight, and the artifacts of the process—meeting minutes, drafts, and emails—are usually filed away and forgotten once the policy has been produced. However, practitioner inquiry brings a spotlight to shine on practice. In this case, the practice in focus was the practice of designing policy through the work of a professional learning community. To this end, the artifacts of this process were given the status of data. Analysis involved contending with this material, dwelling on what would usually be considered ephemera.

ENCOUNTERS WITH CONCEPTS

Categories are the names we give to recognizable patterns or groupings that emerge when we work with data. Sometimes categories are determined in advance. An inquiry question will have one or more categories that have been decided at the design stage (see Chapter 7). For instance, the question "How does explicit teaching of inferencing impact on reading outcomes for grade 4 students?" contains several category terms. One of these is *explicit teaching*. In order to incorporate this term into an inquiry question, we first need to define it. In order to be confident that our data will help answer the question, we will need to collect data that we can predict will give evidence of "explicit teaching." Even what appear to be commonsense terms, such as *child, student, teacher,* or *learning,* become analytical categories when we incorporate them into an inquiry question. A decision to use the term *child* rather than *student,* for instance, may be a conscious choice to consider not only the classroom context but also life outside of school.

However, even when an inquiry has defined its analytical terms from the outset, it is important to keep open to the possibility of new meanings arising that do not fit easily into predetermined categories. Lather (1991) puts it this way:

> Data must be allowed to generate propositions in a dialectical manner that permits the use of a priori theoretical frameworks, but which keeps a particular framework from being the container into which the data must be poured. (p. 267)

So, for instance, an educator may start out with a focus on student engagement. At the outset, the framework may be one that defines a student as either "engaged" or "disengaged" based on behavioral indicators such as time on task. However, if the educator gathers rich observational data of students participating in learning activities over several sessions, then this simple two-part set of categories could well prove to be insufficient. The educator might notice this while reading over observational notes or viewing recordings while thinking about what to name students' modes of participation.

One student might keep his head down over his book and work steadily away until the task is done, while another might spend the first half of a lesson brainstorming approaches with her friends. Is one "engaged" and the other "disengaged"? Or might it be useful to expand the concept to include different ways that students experience and express engagement? Thinking about these different kinds of engagement is an analytical task that can generate new categories. We may wish to distinguish "social engagement" from "individual engagement," for instance.

In Lather's terms, the initial categorization, which established "engagement" and "disengagement" as mutually exclusive opposites, is an "a priori theoretical framework." It is a useful starting point for organizing ideas around an aspect of education. However, such frameworks should not become molds into which data are poured. Instead, inquirers should look for the degree of fit between categories and data and be ready to consider modifying, dropping, or adding to the set of categories used in analysis.

Working with Prior and Emergent Categories

Most of the children at Birchwood Kindergarten enrolled at the colocated Birchwood Primary School when they graduated. The transition process from kindergarten to school was jointly managed by both sites. In the past, the main activity of transition took the form of a half-day school visit by the graduating group of kindergarten children. Informally, the kindergarten staff encouraged children to express their feelings about this change through play and story reading.

Kindergarten director Cynthia had been at Birchwood for over 10 years. She wanted to assist children in making a positive transition to school and she knew that this did not happen in every case. Indeed, recently there seemed to have been an increase in child and parent anxiety about school entry. Cynthia spoke with the head of the junior school about extending the transition program beyond the half-day visit. Her idea was to run visits in reverse, with the new cohort of school entrants returning to spend time with kindergarten children. The idea behind this proposal was that hearing from children a little further on in their school journey would help kindergarten children feel more prepared and less anxious.

The program commenced and the children in reception (prep) at school began weekly visits to the kindergarten during free play time. Cynthia felt that the visits were going well; however, some of the other kindergarten staff expressed concerns. As Cynthia wrote in her report, this prompted her proposal to initiate an inquiry:

> Our interest in looking more deeply into what was occurring during the visits was in part prompted by a challenge from some of our colleagues who had suggested that this regular visiting time could be disadvantaging the kindergarten children who could feel threatened or intimidated by the older children taking over their space. (Meredith, 2006, n.p.)

This inquiry, which was undertaken collaboratively by the kindergarten teaching team, involved gathering multiple kinds of data. These included parent surveys, child interviews, children's drawings, captions dictated by children, and observations of play. Here, we will focus on the analytical process for working with the child data. Our aim is to show how Cynthia worked with both predetermined and emergent categories in order to better understand interactions between primary school and kindergarten children.

In the design phase, the inquiry team had determined to organize observations according to a typology of play that was familiar to many of them. This typology consists of four kinds of play: onlooker, parallel, associative, and cooperative. This reflects a developmental framework that is commonly taught in early childhood teacher training and can be traced back to Parten's research conducted in the 1930s (cited in Santrock, 2007). Thus, it was a highly reputed framework that inquiry team members all recognized as legitimate.

However, when the educators attempted to record children's play observations using this framework as an organizer, it did not work out as they had hoped. Cynthia reported:

> We soon discovered that this plan was not practical to gain data for our inquiry as we missed the more relevant play interactions that were happening around us. So, in line with Freeman's (1998, p. 90) advice, that "changes are part of the research process," we modified our observation methods so that each staff member took time to look for, and critically observe, "play moments." (Meredith, 2006, n.p.)

Staff observations were recorded in descriptive notes and photographic documentation. Rather than applying predetermined categories at the point of observation, the team gathered all the data into a corpus and discussed what they noticed. On the basis of this discussion, they identified the following patterns of interaction:

- Play groups were formed on the basis of attraction to an activity, rather than according to members' ages/stages.
- Children were at times both teachers and learners.
- Children played games with rules that they negotiated and agreed on together.
- Children participated in play by verbally interacting about the play.
- Play was more "concentrated" or "happily intense" during shared visits.

Through this process, new categories of analysis emerged: "activity attraction," "negotiation," "rules," "play talk," "play intensity," and "peer teaching." These categories drew attention to the children's competence as play partners, which had been doubted by some of the kindergarten teachers based on their assumptions about the power relations between the school-children and their younger peers. It also raised a new inquiry question: Why was the play during the shared visits qualitatively different, a difference expressed in the term *happily intense*?

In her report, Cynthia aired one explanation for this, based on the way the shared visits had changed the nature of the boundary between kindergarten and school:

> This inquiry has shown the value of the visiting program from the children's perspective and it has shown that a softening or blurring of the boundaries of school and kindergarten is an overwhelmingly positive experience for young children. Children's development in all areas is individual, therefore, an arbitrary school starting age which does not allow time for children to learn through the play experiences which they have experienced at kindergarten will deny children a basic right to learn through play. (Meredith, 2006, n.p.)

Cynthia's discussion shows the importance of being open to emergent categories. The initial framework of types of play had arisen from developmental theories of childhood. However, bringing together the kindergarten children and schoolchildren in play interactions had "blurred the boundaries" not only between school and kindergarten but also between assumed developmental stages. This gave Cynthia, as an early childhood educator, a means of challenging these assumptions, which had been instrumental in the resistance of some her colleagues to allowing the older children back into the kindergarten.

Constructing the Case

A case is an inquiry construct. Creating a case is an active strategy of meaning-making that can help a practitioner researcher arrive at conclusions about the particular aspect of teaching and learning under focus (Hashweh, 2004). The decision to take a case study approach may be made in the initial design stage or later, at the point of confronting the data. Either way, the case has to be built, and this is an analytical task. Case-based analysis always involves asking: "What is this a case of?" This question "helps teachers to look at a situation and recognize it as an instance of something . . . rather than to see each instance as an isolated event" (Van Es & Sherin, 2008, p. 2).

Building a case involves drawing a boundary around some happening or phenomenon related to an aspect of learning. Deciding what is "in" and what is beyond the boundaries of a case requires careful thought. As Burns (2007) explains:

> [B]ecause actions and interventions in one sphere can have major implications for other spheres, then the way in which we draw the boundaries (to define our

focus of attention) fundamentally affects what we see and how we assess its effectiveness. (p. 22)

Focusing on an individual student is an example. First, there needs to be a reason to select a particular student as a case. Often, this becomes clear after a prior phase of inquiry has established the picture of learning in a particular context, such as a class or course. The student could typify a pattern seen in the larger group or could be exceptional to that pattern. The student might have undergone a change in learning profile. Perhaps, for instance, the student did particularly well in a learning activity when this had not been predicted from his or her track record.

Having selected a focal student, it is then necessary to decide which aspects of the student's participation will be analyzed. The practitioner may have work samples, observational notes, and survey findings. However, it may become necessary to supplement the data with additional material in order to develop a full description and analysis of the student as a learner in this particular context. For instance, peer interactions may emerge as relevant to the case. Some additional observation might generate additional insights into this aspect of participation.

Each kind of data will contribute layers to the case and provide more resources for developing possible explanations of what is happening. As Edwards and Talbot (2014) have written:

> Each case has within it a set of interrelationships that both bind it together and shape it, but also interact with the external world. (p. 126)

So, for instance, in the case of a student, interrelationships could be between the student's self-concept as a learner and the characteristics of the task, or between the teacher's expectations of that student and her or his prior history participating in activities of this kind. Aspects of the external world, or the context surrounding the learning environment, could include curriculum frameworks that structure assessment in a course or the family's access to technology, which is assumed in order to complete homework.

Moving beyond the individual student, practitioners can also find cases in the events of the classroom. This means selecting a learning event or interaction that has given the teacher cause for thought and drawing a boundary around it. Or a site such as a kindergarten, school, or community center might be treated as a case. For educational leaders, an activity could be viewed as a case or a professional group such as a learning community. In each of these situations, the case may be determined in advance or it may develop an identity as a "case of something" through the process of analysis.

It was stated earlier that cases are built. However, a more accurate description might be that case-based analysis tends to move through both deconstructive and reconstructive phases. In the deconstructive phase, something that the practitioner normally experiences in a holistic way (such as a person or a place) becomes fragmented into pieces of data. These fragments command attention in a way that is not usual in everyday practice. For instance, a place that is well known and familiar can become strangely fragmented when it begins to be seen as a case.

This process of deconstruction was experienced by Alison, a primary school teacher, whose inquiry was concerned with the place of Indigenous knowledge in the town's public institutions (Marsh, 2013). She had selected the library as a case of an important public institution, a library used by students in her town. Alison had visited this library many times. For her inquiry, she took many photographs of familiar features, such as shelves of books and displays. Using a digital photo-editing application, she used color coding to underline items relevant to Indigenous knowledge. This made strikingly visible the small number and peripheral position of these resources. By deconstructing the library into visual images and applying a strategy of visual analysis, Alison was ready to describe the library as a case of something: the marginalization of Indigenous knowledge.

In the reconstructive stage of case-based analysis, an integrative method of presenting the case is needed. This may take the form of a written case portrayal, a short documentary film, or a photo story. In the example below, we see how one practitioner used written portrayal to integrate her analysis of several contrastive cases.

Allyson's Case-Based Analysis of Early Childhood Centers: An Integrative Portrayal. Allyson worked as a program director of children's services. Her job involved visiting kindergartens, preschools, and child care centers to evaluate the delivery of educational programs in relation to the national Early Years Learning Framework (EYLF). Allyson had been studying place-based education with a particular focus on the idea of literacies of place (Comber, Nixon, Ashmore, Loo, & Cook, 2006). She had become interested in how the spatial and material characteristics of early childhood settings might impact on their quality as literacy learning environments. She was also concerned with the relationship between these settings and their communities, particularly as the EYLF laid emphasis on partnership with families as essential to effective practice. She framed her inquiry question as, "Do children's services respect and support the place-based literacies of the children and families they serve?" Although this was a closed question (answerable with yes or no), Allyson's approach to inquiring was open. She chose observation and photographic documentation as her main methods of data collection and set out to be as inclusive as possible of relevant aspects of the site's spatial, material, and social qualities.

Allyson spent some time reading through her fieldnotes, viewing her images, and applying various analytic categories, some of which were drawn from her reading and others of which emerged from the data. She then crafted a portrayal for each of the four sites she had studied. Below is one of these portrayals (Dutschke, 2013). This site was one that, prior to embarking on this inquiry, Allyson had considered exemplary. The process of case-based analysis and portrayal writing enabled her to develop a critical, yet appreciative, understanding of the site as a learning environment. Here is her case portrayal:

> This Early Learning Center (ELC) is part of a prestigious all-girl school in the eastern suburbs. Families electing to send their children here for early education and care, are informed of the practices and quality this Reggio Emilia–inspired service observes—that is, a strong artistic focus with a resident art teacher, and utilizing the music and sport resources of the adjoining high school. For many of the children, older siblings have previously attended, and many mothers also attended the school for their formal education; however, once the children start attending the ELC, parents are expected to leave, and have minimal involvement, unless invited. These strong social connections and expectations play a valuable role in the literacies of the children (Edmondson, 2001), representing the community value of social connection, and where academic, artistic, and sporting achievements are prized. The neatness, order, and organization expected by the educators at this service (Prochner, Cleghorn, & Green, 2008) of the children further support the appearance of the tree-lined suburbs, with manicured gardens and neatly maintained homes, and the notion of a structured place and time for play and learning (Neuman & Celano, 2006; Nichols & Nixon, 2013) within the family home.
>
> Exploring this service, children's artwork completed at the service is prominent, as are the celebrations and involvements in school events, through photographic and learning story displays. However, there are few visible signs of connections from within each child's home or culture, and the children are clearly separated from other groups by doors and fences. Important literacies of place for each child appear to be less valued in this environment than the artistic focus, or inspiration, for the service; however, even Malaguzzi, founder of the Reggio Emilia approach, understood that educators "cannot separate [children] from [their] reality. [They] bring these experiences, feelings, and relationships into school with [them]" (Malaguzzi, 1993, p. 1). As Malaguzzi expresses, the place of children in their world—home, family, and culture—needs to be valued and incorporated into the learning and education in which each child participates, for literacies to be more than a social facade.
>
> This may indeed be the challenge for this service, which so eloquently demonstrates the manicured and social environment

around the children, preparing them for later expectations of life (Hicks, 2002), but appears not to see the individual literacies of each child within that environment.

Case portrayals can communicate in a compelling way the nature of an educational issue under investigation. They are not only outcomes of analysis but a powerful means of opening issues for professional dialogue (Hashweh, 2004). In teacher education, richly contextualized accounts of learning environments, interactions, and practices provide authentic challenges to preservice educators (Kim & Hannafin, 2009).

So far, we have considered two kinds of encounters in the analysis dimension of practitioner inquiry: encounters with data and encounters with concepts. We now turn to encounters with the perspectives of others. Of course, all are interrelated; however, collaborative analysis poses its own challenges and offers particular rewards.

ENCOUNTERS WITH THE PERSPECTIVES OF OTHERS: COLLABORATIVE ANALYSIS

Analysis intrinsically involves acts of interpretation, and this means analysts are always taking a view of and on their data. A view always comes from somewhere. That is, to look at our inquiry data, we adopt a perspective. Inquirers' perspectives are informed by their knowledge base, their experience, their assumptions, and their motivations to address a particular problem of educational practice. Discussing the nature of interpretation, Peshkin (2000) writes, "A researcher's self, or identity in a situation, intertwines with his or her understanding of the object of the investigation" (p. 5).

The concept of a community of practice (Wenger, 1998) is commonly invoked when considering collaboration in education (Mackey & Evans, 2011; Owen, 2014). However, there has been a tendency to emphasize shared understandings and common frames of reference. Riveros and colleagues (2012) argue that this emphasis has been used to stifle diversity and mute dissent. When it comes to inquiry, diversity of perspectives is a vital resource for meaning-making. So it is useful to revisit Wenger's original conception of the community of practice and take note of what it has to say about difference. The concept of "partiality" is important here. Each person's perspective gives him or her access to part of a more complex whole. Wenger (1998) explains:

> Mutual engagement involves not only our competence, but also the competence of others. It draws on what we do and what we know, as well as on our ability to connect meaningfully to what we don't do and what we don't know—that is, to the contributions and knowledge of others. In this sense, mutual engagement

is inherently partial; yet, in the context of a shared practice, this partiality is as much a resource as it is a limitation. (p. 76)

The idea that partiality is a resource is a useful one for collaborative inquiry. It means we can accept our limitations as an inevitable aspect of understanding a situation through our own frames of reference. By the same token, we accept the contributions of others, knowing that their perspectives are "partial," but that in collaboration we can build a fuller picture of the situation under investigation. Below are examples of two strategies we have used to foster collaborative analysis in practitioner inquiry contexts.

Data Sharing in the Fishbowl

A fishbowl is a strategy in which a small group of participants agrees to have a focused conversation while being observed by a larger group. A premise of the fishbowl is that educators have access to resources of professional knowledge and experience. These resources are drawn on whenever professionals are asked to make meaning of—interpret—a learning event or product. We have used the fishbowl as a way of encouraging educators to share their in-process thinking about data and artifacts arising from their inquiries. Used in this way, one participant brings to the fishbowl a research artifact and the other participants agree to share their responses, interpretations, and wonderings. The fishbowl session works best when the item of data is limited in size or scope—for example, one or two pieces of student writing, short excerpts from an interview, or a brief video of a classroom activity. Together, the active participants make sense of the data and the observers gain insights into how such collaboration works in practice.

The fishbowl session is structured in three stages:

- *First impressions.* The focus practitioner briefly states the topic of the inquiry and presents the data to the group, without making any further comment. Each group member in turn shares his or her first impressions of the data. The focus practitioner listens, preferably without responding.
- *Contextualizing the data.* The focus practitioner now gives information about the context for the data—for example, the instructions for a writing task, the achievement profile of the student, the characteristics of the survey cohort, or the demographic profile of the community from which interviewees were drawn. The fishbowl group now reconsiders the data in light of this information. The focus practitioner listens to the interpretations of the group members and answers any further questions.
- *Reflection on the process.* The focus practitioner reflects on whether and how the perspectives and questions of his or her peers have

contributed new insights into to his or her interpretation of the data. Other group members reflect on their participation. Observers share their responses to the activity.

To illustrate this process, we will look at an example of the fishbowl in practice. The focus practitioner in this case was Faye, a special-needs educator, inquiring into digital word processing by students with low literacy in the early years of elementary school. In the fishbowl with Faye were Nick and Hamish, both primary/elementary teachers, and Rosa, a literacy specialist.

Faye's inquiry question was, "Will using the computer make a difference to a grade 3 student's literacy skills, making them comparable to those of her peers?" Faye brought two pieces of writing completed by the case study student, both typed on a computer. The first was a draft of a letter and included the teacher's written comments and revision marks. The second was the student's final copy. The draft included a hand-drawn picture while the second had no visual element.

Below are some excerpts from discussion at the first impression stage, highlighting the different perspectives participants brought to their initial decontextualized interpretation of the data:

Rosa: There is control over high-frequency words. Three-letter phonetics are correct. But if the child can master *dear* and *love*, why is she reverting to single-letter words? Single-letter words represent an earlier phase.

Nick: "w-e" could be the word *we*. "r w e" could be email shorthand.

Hamish: This child has had exposure to the letter genre.

Rosa made the most extensive contribution to the discussion at this stage, drawing on her interpretive repertoire as a literacy specialist. Referencing a developmental model of literacy, she found the data puzzling. A child who is able to write three- and four-letter words should not be including single letters that are not obviously words, such as "r."

Nick offered another possible explanation for the appearance of the single letter "r." He referenced his knowledge of text conventions for digital text in which single letters can stand for whole words. Thus, the succession of single letters (r-w-e) might stand for the expression "are we." Hamish had less to say but contributed a different perspective, focusing his attention on the genre features of the text.

Faye now offered contextual information regarding the data:

The data were produced on the last day of the term. The intention of the email to Mum was to encourage the student to practice her writing. It was her first attempt at writing an email by herself. Previously they had been scribed. This text was exceptional compared to her previous work. This child could not even spell her name before this. It's the first time she had put spaces between words.

The discussion in the fishbowl now turned to the nature of, and possible explanations for, this improvement. A key issue was whether the improvement was in IT (information technology) skills primarily, or in literacy, or both.

Hamish: Have you reflected on the improvement in IT literacy?
Faye: Yes. Email is only one component of what she can do. This child is now teaching other children how to use the computer.
Rosa: I'm puzzled. One concern is: She's emailed Mum how many times? Is it always a similar message?
Faye: Each time we try to put a new little message in.
Rosa: IT is hugely improved, but in terms of core literacy, could she just be parroting? If the literacy is really building, would we see starting *you* with an "r"? Are we seeing underlying growth or is it confidence?
Faye: It is confidence, but some of these small steps are big things. She's never made a beginning before.
Nick: I'd be measuring the child's improvement rather than comparing her to the rest of the group.

Faye was being challenged by her peers. Hamish suggested that improvement in IT skills should also be considered alongside literacy. Rosa, on the other hand, was clearly suspicious as to whether the data could be counted as evidence of a genuine improvement in literacy. She suggested that the change in the child's writing did not show "underlying growth," reflecting the strength of a developmental model in her interpretive repertoire.

These challenges worked to encourage Faye to develop her account of the child's improvement to produce a fuller picture of her learning. Within this account, she included confidence as a significant change, as well as the child's new expert status with her peers. Thus, the shift from handwritten text to digital writing, and from classroom exercises to authentic communication with a family member, could be seen as having multiple outcomes.

In the reflection, Faye said she found the questions "very helpful" and that they prompted her to think, "What am I looking at?" As she listened to her peers and answered their questions, she had "come to a new framing of the question." Whereas initially she had intended to compare the child's progress to the progress of her peers, she now intended to focus on the child's participation in email communication from the perspective of how this made a difference to her learning.

The aim of the fishbowl is not to come to a consensus. In the reflection, Rosa continued to push for "more objective measures" and one of the observers suggested that "the two pieces of work should be a similar size to facilitate quantitative comparison." These are epistemological debates about the nature of evidence. We suggest that it is constructive for educators to participate in these debates, whichever position they occupy. For Faye, becoming aware of the various possible readings of her data helped her reconsider her own interpretations. It also gave her a sense of how an audience of peers might respond to her argument, which encouraged her to build a strong rationale for her conclusions.

Collaborative Case Building

Earlier in this chapter, we considered the nature of the case as an important construct in analysis. Here, we will describe how supported peer collaboration can be an effective means of developing the skills of case-based analysis. Below is an example of how this can work in practice. The participants in this particular activity were undertaking graduate studies and came from a range of educational practice backgrounds. Some were classroom practitioners, some were educational leaders, and others had educational roles in allied services, such as health and community development. The group met during a weeklong summer intensive dedicated to research development that was led by the first author.

First, the group was introduced to the concept of the case, similar to the definition given above. Then they were asked to form groups of three or four, which would be their teams for the next few days whenever the case study activity was being undertaken. The project, as explained to the participants, was as follows:

> You will be given a set of data concerning a particular grade 9 student, "Rick." Rick was selected by his teacher as a "boy of concern" in relation to his participation in literacy learning. You will also be provided with some statements that are indicative of theoretical and research perspectives on the subjects of literacy and gender. Your task is to develop a portrayal of the case of Rick, based on your analysis of the case study data, which will be presented on the final day. This portrayal must attempt to explain Rick's participation in literacy and develop some recommendations for effective work with him. This is a collaborative analysis activity, which should draw on the interpretive resources of all group members. Please keep in mind Griffiths (1998) on research

collaboration from a social justice perspective—as research "with" rather than "on." She argues that collaboration must involve:

- taking on board others' perspectives,
- taking these perspectives seriously enough to be influenced by them, and
- working together to implement action.

If a practitioner has never produced a case portrayal before, it can be helpful to see one or more examples. For this activity, a model of a case portrayal was provided to the participants (Nichols, 2003) and is reproduced in part below. This example was taken from the first author's research on children's transition from preschool to school. Given that the participants were engaged in graduate study, the model was appropriate to the kind of research writing they were preparing to produce.

The Case of Prudence from Preschool to School

Prudence's story is interesting for what it can tell us about connections and disjunctures between school literacy and children's social experience. Although this issue has been raised many times in the past, it has generally been in relation to what are often called "diverse communities"—in other words, where there is an obvious social class or cultural difference between families and the school system (Au, 1997; Singh, 2001). However, other kinds of pressures can also produce disjunctures that impact on children's literacy learning. In the current climate, with an increasing emphasis on measurable literacy outcomes from the early years, the very practices that are intended to ensure such outcomes can mitigate against children drawing on their social experiences and, thus, produce disconnections even for children one would expect to be advantaged (Nichols, 2003).

This portrayal begins with a clear definition of the case of Prudence as a "case of something" (Van Es & Sherin, 2008). It establishes the broader phenomenon under inquiry as the transition from preschool to school. It acknowledges the generally accepted view of the main cause of problematic transition—that is, disjuncture between the student's home/community context and the context of school. It then asserts that new problems of transition are being caused by the move to measurable outcomes in literacy assessment, creating obstacles to children drawing on their social experiences. Prudence thus appears as a member of a new group of children facing disjunctures in transition not for reasons of cultural diversity, but owing to the pressure of performance in literacy assessment. The case of Prudence has been established in general terms, and now the specific quality of her experience can be considered.

The practitioner group could see where they were heading in terms of an outcome. They were then given a set of data on Rick. Each data set included the following:

- An excerpt from an interview with Rick
- An excerpt from an interview with Rick's teacher
- The teacher's observational fieldnotes of Rick in class
- Rick's own observations of the class
- Two assignments written by Rick
- Completed assessment rubrics for both assignments

One team for this activity consisted of three practitioners—an elementary school principal, a guidance counselor, and a health educator. They spent some time discussing all the data and making descriptive notes and summaries. The educators in this group all subscribed to a strength-based approach in their professional practice and agreed on the principle that every student has strengths that should be drawn on in their learning. Taking this inquiry stance, they actively looked for Rick's strengths, based on his own statements, his work samples, the teacher's comments, and the teacher's observations. They also acknowledged both Rick's and the teacher's critiques and concerns.

The group then considered the differences and potential contradictions that arose when data were juxtaposed. They noted, for instance, that Rick's teacher described him as impulsive, unsettled, and prone to making errors on assignments. They considered these comments in light of Rick's description of his interactions with his cricket coach, from whom he not only welcomed but sought out critical feedback so that he could improve his technique.

In recording their thoughts, the group indicated when they were uncertain and remained open to different interpretations. For instance, the note "bragging or expecting punishment?" was recorded to indicate two possible interpretations of Rick's statement about skipping a detention. At one point, the group listed adjectives that had been, or could be, used to describe Rick. The picture that emerged was complex and contradictory: *impulsive, aggressive, sporty, cooperative, alert, attention-seeking, team player, antisocial, encouraging, fascinating.*

In working toward their portrayal, the group determined that a consensus on Rick was not useful. Glossing over these differences in experiences of and beliefs about Rick would not generate an explanation for the situation in which Rick found himself at school. In this, they were consistent with the approach of Bennett and Elman (2006), who argue that within-case analysis "may provide evidence that bears on multiple testable implications of a theory" (p. 459). Instead, they decided to model the important relationships they could see in the data. The diagrammatic representation they produced can be seen in Figure 8.1.

This model reflects that Rick's experiences of learning occurred in more than one context, and that these contexts enabled different competencies and learner identities. The model shows that Rick and his teacher may agree on aspects of his learner identity. This is seen in the data when the teacher refers to Rick as cooperative, which is also reflected in Rick's self-described relationship with his coach. However, it also shows that some of Rick's dispositions to learning, because they are triggered outside of the classroom, may not be available to his teacher. She therefore must rely on her observations of Rick's classroom behavior to draw her conclusions about him as a learner.

This holistic analysis allows for the generation of new insights about Rick's learning. The group applied the model back to reinterpreting one of Rick's assignments. This task, undertaken in religion studies, asked students to describe a hero; according to his teacher's assessment, this was one of Rick's more successful activities. The teacher interpreted Rick's hero description as indicating he had "picked something up" from the classwork, which had focused on Jesus as a hero and had encouraged students to critique popular culture and sporting heroes.

Using this model, the group members argued in their presentation that this task had enabled Rick to positively draw on his out-of-school experiences to develop a hero description that not only aligned with the curriculum

Figure 8.1. Model Produced Through Collaborative Case Analysis

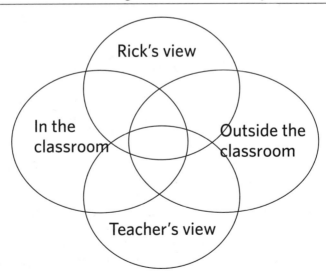

agenda but was subjectively authentic to Rick. However, far from being a reflection of his teacher's anti-sports stance, these heroic characteristics aligned with Rick's description of his coach, who represented the kind of selfless and fair sportsman Rick himself aspired to be. Thinking through the implications of this analysis for creating a better school experience and outcomes for Rick, the group decided to draw on the coach role to make recommendations. In their presentation, the members of the group argued for:

> continuing to tell Rick how to improve like a coach, showing him how to improve, giving him more chance to practice, staying engaged with him, "having faith," not "having a go at him."

Given that Rick is a case "of something," these recommendations were not specifically directed at Rick's teacher. Rather, they were framed as relevant to all teachers who find students like Rick in their classes.

CONCLUSION

We have argued that analysis in practitioner inquiry is a process of layering involving three kinds of encounters: with data, with concepts, and with the perspectives of others. Indeed, the concept of layering comes from an educator who, responding anonymously to our IPI survey, wrote: "It was very much a layering, and it is very much in the reflection that you understand the significance of [an inquiry]."

Practitioner inquiry is often described as a linear process in which analysis is a stage following data collection and preceding reporting. When a busy teacher has a tight deadline to prepare an inquiry report for her graduate course, analysis might be experienced in just this way. "Oh heck, what am I going to do with all this data?" may well be the question asked at 11:00 P.M., when the marking is finished and inquiry time begins.

However, as our anonymous teacher has written, "It is very much in the reflection that you understand." Making time to dwell with data, to allow them to make an impression, to think about them in terms of concepts, to wonder whether a case is in the process of being built, to put one's tentative impressions out there and open ourselves to others' interpretations—all these acts help layer our analysis. As we have seen from the examples of educators whose analytic activities are shared in this chapter, thoughtful analysis genuinely produces new knowledge about educational issues of importance. This analysis enables educators to argue for change.

McLaughlin and O'Brien-Strain (2008) found this when, as university academics, they worked with schools and community groups to share data and develop inquiries about at-risk youth. They had worked hard to encourage these separate groups to share their data and collaborate in analyzing those data to develop greater insight into the experiences of young people. On the basis of this experience, they argued that

> changes as the result of data integration is achieved not through the data itself but rather by creating a structure for building relationships and knowledge. (McLaughlin & O'Brien-Strain, 2008, p. 314)

As facilitators of inquiry, we have attempted to build this structure in partnership with educators. Modeling of analytical strategies, provision of examples, and facilitation of collaborative analysis, such as in the fishbowl, are some of the strategies we have used. Most of all, we have tried to embody and demonstrate respect—respect for the data, respect for ideas, and respect for others' insights, both as participants and as collaborators. As our interpretive repertoires expand, our collective ability to understand the complexities of learning and teaching, and to intervene thoughtfully, is strengthened.

CHAPTER 9

Conclusion

This book set out to answer the question: What are the impacts of practitioner inquiry? In addressing this question, we have often come up against the complexities of the change process that is implied by the term *impact*. Often, as we read and pored over the reports of inquiries and the surveys and interviews we conducted, we were reminded of the multiple and contradictory issues at play for practitioners as they ponder what to do, especially for students causing them concern. The subtlety of these processes and the calculations at play stood in contrast to the policy pronouncements promoting educational change and reform in which "evidence-based" practices are laid out as if ready to be picked up and plugged into the classroom with inevitably successful results. We came to understand that whatever model is deployed for understanding change determines what can be recognized as "success" and structures the accounts of how change might be achieved in educational systems.

We begin, then, with a discussion of the nature of impacts, given the kinds of professional work worlds to which the practitioners were brave and kind enough to give us access through their reports, as well as understanding our own context as practitioners. This is the first key insight we draw from the work of this book. We propose that the impacts of practitioner inquiry are best understood by conceptualizing education contexts as complex systems rather than as hierarchical structures. Second, the way that the practitioners work in inquiries has led us to think differently about accountability, and thus to recognize the ways in which practitioner inquiry supports professional accountability. Our third insight into impacts is that deep, critical thinking is the key driver of impactful inquiry. Yet we caution against consensus models of professional community. Fourth, we turn to the issue of teacher leadership as an orientation developed through the public, collegial dimension of inquiry. Finally, we consider debates about the relative nature and status of practitioner inquiry and academic research and challenge the view that the worlds of practice and theory create different and incommensurable expertise.

TO UNDERSTAND IMPACTS,
THINK COMPLEX NETWORKED SYSTEMS

The unpredictable and dynamic impacts of inquiring practitioners in the classroom, school, and profession are much better explained by networking and complexity models than linear hierarchical models. A school can be thought of as a space of flows: Bodies, talk, ideas, practices, and objects are always in motion, even when to the inexperienced eye all that can be seen are students sitting in rows. This is why Reilly (2009) directs us to look "in the flow of dynamic encounters" for professional learning in action (p. 94). Teachers and students are habitués of this space and are attuned to the moment-by-moment opportunities to direct, intervene, or rechannel flows. We have argued that one of the ways in which inquiring practitioners positively affect their schools' learning cultures is through catching "teachable moments" with colleagues (see Chapter 3), just as they change the dynamic in the classroom by making on-the-spot decisions about how to challenge a student.

Examining educational reform through the lens of complexity theory, Snyder (2013) compares three ways of thinking about educational problems and solutions: the simple, the complicated, and the complex. Simple problems can be clearly defined in terms of direct cause-and-effect relationships. When starting out as inquirers, educators may begin with this kind of problem framing. Complicated problems are those in which relationships between causes and effects can be arrived at by applying appropriate analytic methods to a suitable data set. However, according to Snyder, educational problems are often treated as complicated when they would be better understood as complex. The realm of the complex is "a space of constant flux and unpredictability" in which "[t]here are no right answers, only emergent behaviors" (Snyder, 2013, p. 8). The examples provided of practitioner research projects in Chapters 5 and 6 (Inclusive Education Project and Boys' Literacies Project, respectively) illustrate how practitioner inquiry can operate in a zone of complexity in fields that continue to challenge education systems and workers. To optimize an education system's ability to address complex problems, there is a need for "safe spaces for patterns to emerge, which is best done by increasing levels of interaction and communication" (Snyder, 2013, p. 9). Writing about strategic change, Stacey (1995) notes that an organization becomes changeable:

> when its informal network system, consisting of self-organizing patterns of connections between people within and across its boundaries, is richly connected enough to operate on the edge of instability, where it produces ever-changing emergent patterns of behavior. (p. 489)

This suggests that practitioner inquiry can assist education systems to address complex problems to the extent that across a system, it opens up multiple "safe spaces" within which interactions center on understanding patterns across participants' sites of practice.

TEACHERS ENACT ACCOUNTABILITY THROUGH INQUIRY

One of the key rationales for systemic education reform under neoliberal political governments has been that teachers must be forced to assume responsibility for student learning outcomes (Welner & Mathis, 2015). When the No Child Left Behind Act (NCLB) was instituted in the United States in 2002, then federal education advisor Susan Neuman announced that it would "stifle and hopefully kill" what she described as "creative and experimental teaching methods" (Balta, 2002). In Australia, the context for studies presented here, a powerful conservative lobby with vocal media spokespersons characterized teachers as a generation of free-thinking hippie relics, careless of any concern for the nation's performance on international tests (Bessant, 2011).

Analyzing the implementation of National Board for Professional Teaching Standards, Anagnostopoulos and colleagues (2010) identify two "competing logics" of educational accountability: "a technical expertise logic resting on instrumental appeals and market-based validation . . . and a social trustee logic resting on moral appeals that link professional knowledge to the public good" (p. 341). The technical expertise logic has been uppermost in reforms based on the specification of particular teaching methods linked to the use of mandated curriculum resources, as in NCLB (Handsfield, Crumpler, & Dean, 2010). However, it is the moral logic that resonates more strongly with the motivations of the educators whose experiences form the basis of this book. We would include ourselves in that number.

These educators' sense of responsibility for their students aligns with what O'Day (2002) describes as "professional accountability," an orientation that "plac[es] the needs of the clients (students) at the center of professional work" (p. 316). This ethic of care does not translate into a generalized goal of raising average test scores in a class or school by a few points. Rather, it is most active when challenged by the struggles, resistance, or withdrawal of particular students. It is these students who make educators want to do better. Recall the teachers who joined the Inclusive Education Project (Chapter 5). Many of them had been assigned to the most challenging students early in their careers. Their determination to succeed and their gradual realization of the untapped potential of these marginalized students drove them to keep trying strategies, resources, and different ways of being an educator.

Improvement reforms based on this kind of professional accountability, rather than on top-down bureaucratic accountability, have the following characteristics:

[T]hey generate and focus attention on information relevant to teaching and learning, motivate individuals and schools to use that information and expend effort to improve practice, build the knowledge base necessary for interpreting and applying new information to improve practice, and allocate resources for all of the above. (O'Day, 2002, p. 295)

We argue that practitioner inquiry is an ideal fit for professional accountability seeking such outcomes. It focuses educators' attention on practice, strengthens their knowledge base, generates resources, and connects with the most powerful motivator for teachers: their sense of responsibility to students.

DEEP, CRITICAL THINKING IS THE ENGINE FOR IMPACTFUL INQUIRY

Impactful practitioner inquiry is as much conceptual as it is practical. Educators find inquiries impactful when they challenge themselves to think and speak differently about their practice, their students, the curriculum, and the nature of teaching and learning. This has long been the goal of practitioner inquiry in the critical tradition (Cochran-Smith & Lytle, 1990; Cochran-Smith & Lytle, 1999; Kemmis, 2010; Lytle & Cochran-Smith, 1992). Underlying this view of inquiry is the understanding that "what counts as knowledge" in education—whether this be in a kindergarten, school, or university context—can never be fully determined by those outside the process; it is always "inevitably negotiate[d]" (Cochran-Smith & Lytle, 1993, p. 45). Critical inquiry involves interrogating how teachers and students "construct and reconstruct the curriculum" (Lytle & Cochran-Smith, 1992, p. 458).

This conceptual work is driven by divergence, debate, and dialogue much more than consensus. This recognition addresses a critique of practitioner inquiry (PI) as simply giving teachers "'permission' to follow their instincts" (McWilliam, 2004, p. 122). Throughout this book, we have described situations in which happenings in schools and classrooms were opened up to questioning, analysis, and reconceptualization. This can only happen if divergent views and alternative explanations are allowed into the inquiry space. Inquiry's questioning of educational business as usual opens up a space from which a new stance can be taken.

One way to think of this process is in terms of discourse theory—the concept of discourse as a configuration that brings together ways of speaking, ways of thinking, and ways of doing (Gee, 1990). Discourse, as Lemke (1990) explains, "is a mode of social action. It is not just language, but language-in-use in a community" (p. 208). Education is a discursive field within which exists a number of ways of defining, problematizing, and structuring educational action. This has always been the case, and is certainly a strong feature of the field in the current context. Case studies of trainee and early career teachers have shown that the process of developing a teacher identity involves negotiating these competing versions of the truth about teaching (Miller Marsh, 2002). Considering one such case, Jackson (2001) makes reference to competing discourses:

> [K]nowledge of more than one discourse and the recognition that meaning is plural allows for a measure of choice on the part of the individual, and even where choice is not available, resistance is possible. (p. 304)

When divergent views are brought into an inquiry space, then the potential exists for alternative discourses to be offered, tested, and possibly taken up. When an educator acquires an alternative discourse, questions can be asked from within this discourse that can help practitioners look with fresh eyes at what seem to be intractable problems. Without such questioning, dominant discourses can simply be reinstated, even when considerable effort is made to resource and encourage educational innovation (Thomson, Hall, & Jones, 2013). From this perspective, we caution against too great an emphasis on achieving common language and purpose, such as the use of a "collectively held standard of teaching quality" as a means by which professional learning communities can judge the practices of their members (Darling-Hammond & Richardson, 2009, p. 50). Diversity of perspectives, and a rich ecology of practices, is the best environment in which to promote improved education for all.

INQUIRY DEVELOPS IMPACTFUL LEADERS

New models of teacher and curriculum leadership have emerged that seek to recognize the potential of skilled classroom practitioners to strengthen the profession, without requiring them to leave the classroom in order to take up leadership opportunities (Dawson, 2011). Staying connected to practice is very important for educators, even those who leave the classroom, as is clear from the experiences shared in this book. Through their participation in inquiry, many have found themselves taking up new roles that extend their expertise into working with colleagues in and across sites to improve practice.

Practitioner inquiry maintains a central focus on practice while adding to the educator's repertoire of skills and orientations that support a leadership trajectory. This trajectory is no doubt reinforced when the definition of educational leadership explicitly includes the practice of research or inquiry. This is the case in Australia, where a track record in teacher research is one of the indicators that a proficient teacher is ready for lead teacher status (AITSL, 2011). However, even when teacher standards do not include inquiry, they often highlight competencies that are closely linked to inquiry skills and orientations, such as critical thinking, reflective practice, and lifelong learning (CEPPE, 2013).

It is often noted that teaching is an isolating practice, which is constituted as such by the curriculum and spatial architecture of schooling (Lawn, 1999; Miller, 2005). However, the esteem of peers is very important to educators, and this can have both positive and negative effects (McWilliam & Singh, 2004). A closed-door culture in schools can reinforce a normative social environment in which neither failures nor successes are explored in sufficient detail for others to learn from them (Dawson, 2011). Though there are many models of collegial interaction, practitioner inquiry is distinctive for valuing a form of public reporting that invites response (Altrichter, Posch, & Somekh, 1993; Lankshear & Knobel, 2004). Our analysis has shown how experience in practitioner inquiry, particularly when findings are publicly shared with colleagues, gives an educator a position from which it is possible to consider leadership. As one of our IPI educators told us: "Somebody beside the students valued what I had done." This sense of being valued outside the classroom, as well as within it, is highly motivating for educators. Cameron and Lovett (2015) found that among a cohort of educators deemed "highly promising," those who were most satisfied 9 years into their careers were supported by principals to take on "extended roles" in "collective work with teachers" (p. 159). The opportunity for challenge and extension, which is associated with the recognition of potential, can transform teachers' identities, from just coping to possessing the confidence to continually take on challenges.

Recognition, and the chance to step out of the classroom, is particularly important for teachers trying to make a difference in the toughest circumstances. Schools have a tendency to group their most challenging students—through streaming or other forms of differentiation—and allocate these students to the least experienced or most transient teachers. We saw this in Chapter 5, from the accounts of the teachers in the Inclusive Education Project. For many of these teachers, their inquiry experience was the first time they had encountered a peer audience with whom to share their successes and get feedback on their plans. Years later, one of these educators, Gemma, moved on to a series of acting deputy roles. After each of these roles, she chose to step back into the classroom. She explains:

> I haven't gone up, I've gone under, but I'm actually having fun
> managing up, getting leadership to change its model and perspective
> rather than them changing the other way down, and that is fun. . . .
> In order to do that, it has to be based on the concept of respect and
> understanding of the knowledge and the skill that you bring, not from
> the identity, from labeled positions, which tends to be the hierarchical
> model we work in.

The metaphor of a trajectory is perhaps too linear for inquiring practitioners like Gemma. Moving up within the hierarchy has held no interest for her, although having an influence on leadership certainly has. Perhaps *career tapestry* would be a better term for this pattern of moving between classroom and leadership contexts of practice. Importantly, Gemma identifies the basis of her influence as "knowledge and skill" rather than position, and she directly attributes practitioner inquiry as contributing to her knowledge, practice, and reputation.

CHALLENGING THE BINARY MODEL OF RESEARCH AND PRACTICE

A number of scholars have attempted to distinguish inquiry and research as qualitatively different and, often, as complementary endeavors in an overall goal of improving educational outcomes. Labaree (2008) is typical of this group, differentiating the goals and roles of educators on the one hand and researchers on the other. He characterizes teachers as "primarily engaged in a practice of social improvement, grounded in personal relationships with particular students," whereas researchers are "primarily [engaged] in a practice of social analysis, grounded in intellectual conceptions of education generalized across contexts" (p. 421). These different roles and goals support different kinds of knowledge production and, thus, expertise: While teachers' knowledge is "largely an accumulation of clinical experiences," researchers' knowledge is "largely a web of theories" (p. 421). Labaree (2008) calls for a "fruitful dialogue between practitioners in the two zones" (p. 422).

Note that in this view, one's knowledge is a function of one's context (either embedded in practice or floating above it in the pure air of social theory). This means that a practitioner could never, by virtue of this role, engage in social analysis. However, this leaves open the possibility that a practitioner could transition out of practice into academia and, thus, have the opportunity to become a researcher. Although this could explain the trajectories of the authors of this book, to this proposition we respond in the negative. Neither of us left our teacher identities behind when we became academics (which was a gradual process rather than a sudden career switch). If the imagined "fruitful dialogue" between practitioners and researchers were to be enacted, we would be in the unsettling situation of having to bounce back and forth between sides. A teacher habitus, once acquired, is ingrained and unshakeable (Wright, 2008); it is reactivated every time one steps into a classroom, whether as an educator or researcher. Also, the work of teacher training is an educational practice. We are practitioners of teacher education and this book is, in part, an outcome of our own practitioner inquiry.

The model of research in which exponents construct "a web of theo-ries," existing somehow above or outside the everyday contexts of practice, also excludes a significant body of educational research. In our own field of expertise, literacy, some of the most important studies have taken the form of ethnographic or qualitative case study designs. Shirley Brice Heath's (1983) landmark ethnographic study made visible the foundation of school-like "ways" built in middle-class homes before children entered school, as well as the different, socially valuable but less advantageous "ways" learned in African American and poor White communities. Michael Halliday's (1978) alternative to traditional grammar—systemic functional linguistics—which is now the basis of language curricula worldwide, was developed through a painstaking, in-depth study of his own child's language development from birth. These are just two examples of studies that generated theories that have been subsequently applied by generations of researchers, and were de-veloped out of contextualized, sustained engagement in which the research-ers were participants.

When we consider the contributions of engaged, immersed researchers such as these, a divide between researchers and practitioners based on a view of research as disengaged and decontextualized is no longer sustain-able. Teachers' engagement in a context does not disqualify them from the role of researcher. It is rarely remembered that Heath's (1983) co-research-ers were teachers who were also undertaking graduate study with her dur-ing her research project. Heath's insights about middle-class literacy ways, about school literacy ways, and about the patterned nature of these ways across contexts were drawn from the observations, reflections, and analysis of these inquiring educators.

Rather than the singular subjects of "university researcher" and "prac-titioner," we suggest that all educators and researchers occupy multiple sub-jectivities. There is no such thing as "the practitioner"—there are educators with expertise in middle school mathematics, play-based learning, behav-ior management, fostering creativity, literacy coaching, parent engagement, teacher development, and many more areas of practice. Educators' careers take them through many contexts and involve taking up roles in and out of classrooms and in different school communities. Even from the start of their training, preservice educators find themselves negotiating professional identities that differ from one classroom to the next (Jackson, 2001). In the career of an educator, funds of knowledge (Moll, 1990) grow as they are activated in many different contexts, with different classes of children or staffs of colleagues. These layers of experience are integral to the interpre-tive repertoires that educators, regardless of their contexts of practice, bring to the act of inquiry. For ourselves, professional identities include classroom teacher, subject-area exponent, teacher educator, literacy researcher, educa-tional administrator, colleague, and writer. Each of these identities is linked to knowledge acquired through practice. These multiple identities can be in tension, as we attempt to draw on classroom teacher practice knowledge when others would prefer to locate us in an imagined "ivory tower." Such tensions can be felt as intrapersonal struggles and sources of productive uncertainty.

In the model of research where practitioners and researchers take on "complementary" roles, both have their own specific knowledge to contribute to a broader understanding of education. Because their knowledge bases are considered different in kind, it is hard to see how either could challenge the other in any meaningful way. Rather, each would be allocated the right to add a piece to the puzzle—the "practice piece" or the "theory piece." This does not at all match our experience of the kinds of conversations and working interactions in which we have participated when co-researching with educators from school or early childhood sites of practice. Any group of educators potentially has access to the combined knowledge resources of its members. That is part of the power of collaboration in inquiry. Exposure to others' knowledge resources helps expand the interpretive repertoires of all collaborating inquirers. When a climate of trust and openness is established, challenges come from all quarters and are engaged and contested, regardless of whether the person is speaking as a school-based or a university-based inquirer.

We are aware that working across the identities of educator and researcher can be complicated and unsettling. In a study of teachers who had undertaken an action research course, Toope (2008) noted identity tensions experienced by one of the teachers:

> Within the teacher research program, Kate was positioned as a knower—as a teacher researcher she was encouraged to claim her knowledge. Within her school, Kate has to discipline herself not to reveal her knowing subject. These contradictory discourses mean Kate has to work hard at managing disparate forms of subjectivities to be "in synch." (p. 286)

The dominant discourse in Kate's school is one with which we are familiar. This discourse regards teacher knowledge as the accumulation of contextualized practical experience and positions "theory" as coming from outside practice. As a newcomer to her school, Kate was positioned as one who had not yet accumulated sufficient experience to be counted as a "knower."

Joining a practitioner community, educators encounter alternative ways of talking and thinking about teaching in which the educator is positioned as a questioner, inquirer, and knowledge producer. For some, this means acquiring a new form of subjectivity, one in which the status of knower is not dependent on length of service at a particular school or on maintaining the status quo. The ability to survive in a system, however, still relies on the ability to take up and use the terms of the system's dominant discourses

(Thomson, Hall, & Jones, 2013). So practitioner inquirers do not cease to be adept at implementing policy. Similarly, our own subscription to flexible learning models in higher education has not made us immune to the dictates of a performance management regime. From this perspective, whether one is a university-based educator or a school-based researcher, the ability to manage multiple identities is integral to sustaining a professional life.

CONCLUSION

Our investigations into the impact of practitioner inquiry show that the work of reform and improvement in education is multilayered, complex, and site-sensitive. Our informants have shown us that practitioners are willing to play a significant role in reform processes, including taking leadership, if they can participate fully in all its challenges—intellectually, ethically, as well as practically. Practitioner inquiry is an approach uniquely equipped to assist in this process because it engages in all these challenges and has the potential to promote well-considered change. For the practitioner researchers with whom we worked, well-considered change involves considering its impact on their students, especially those who are most challenged by current practice. Such an enterprise is never completed, as exhibited by the practitioners involved in multiple projects. Answering questions leads to further challenges and new uncertainties, a situation that inquiring practitioners expect and embrace.

Impacts of Practitioner Inquiry Survey

INTRODUCTION

The purpose of this survey is to explore how your involvement in practitioner inquiry has impacted your professional practice and career in positive, negative, or other ways. We will use the results of this survey to better inform school systems, universities, and others who support and sponsor teacher research about the benefits (as well as the drawbacks) of this work, and to provide advice about how best to plan and support practitioner inquiry projects.

Definition of Practitioner Inquiry in Education

Practitioner inquiry involves educational practitioners engaging in systematic inquiry into aspects of their practice (at individual, worksite, or even systems levels), the results of which are made public in some way (for example, through reports, conference presentations, workshops).

Although practitioner inquiry may involve other professionals such as university researchers or system leaders, practitioners play a significant role in one or more of these: establishing research questions, designing research, generating data, analyzing data, and reporting on findings.

There are many contexts for, and initiators of, practitioner inquiry. For example, practitioner inquiry may be part of an accredited university course; it may be initiated and funded by a worksite or system; or it may be conducted by a small group of teachers on their own initiative.

This survey has five sections:

Section A asks which practitioner inquiry projects you have been involved in.
Section B considers what inquiry practices were involved in those projects.
Section C looks at the impacts that your involvement has had on your professional practice and your career.
Section D asks you to consider which projects have had the most significant impacts.
Section E requests some basic statistical information about you and asks if you are interested in participating in a follow-up interview.

Privacy

This is an anonymous survey, unless you elect to provide us with your name in Section E. Even if you provide your name for a possible interview follow-up, your identity will not be revealed in the reporting of the findings from the survey.

SECTION A—PRACTITIONER INQUIRY PROJECTS

In this section, we want to find out about the kinds of projects you have been involved in over the past 10 years. If you have been involved in more than five projects, please choose those that have been most significant to you.

1. Project Topics

List the inquiry projects you've worked in over the past 10 years, by topic or title.

Please tell us which years each project ran in and indicate your position within the school at the time.

	Title or topic of project	Years undertaken	Position held at time (e.g., teacher, principal, head of science, counselor, etc.)
Project 1			
Project 2			
Project 3			
Project 4			
Project 5			

2. Project Scope

Please describe each project (large or small) using the table below. Tick as many boxes as apply to each.

Single-teacher project: Initiated by you and run completely within your own class/ practice

School-level project: Initiated at the school level and run completely within one school (by more than one teacher)

Network-level project: Initiated and run by your school system and involving more than one school

Partnership project: Run by a university and your school system and involving a network of schools

	Single-teacher project	School-level project	Network-level project	Partnership project	Undertaken for university accreditation
Project 1					
Project 2					
Project 3					
Project 4					
Project 5					

3. Previous Projects

This survey asks you to focus on your involvement in practitioner inquiry projects over the past 10 years. However, you may have been involved in projects prior to this time that had a significant impact on you. If this applies to you, please indicate briefly any involvement in significant inquiry prior to this period.

SECTION B—INQUIRY PRACTICES

In this section, we explore the kinds of research or inquiry practices that were involved in the projects you undertook during the past 10 years. By *inquiry practices*, we mean any research practices involved in the conduct of a project from its initial stages right through to reporting. We've listed the most common practices under headings related to typical project stages, but we've also left room for you to write in additional ones.

4. Inquiry Practices You Have Undertaken

Please indicate which inquiry practices you undertook in the course of those projects listed in question 1.

A. Project design and development
I developed my research question/objectives
I negotiated my research question/objectives as part of a team
I had my research question/objectives developed by another
My project was built on academic and/or professional reading
My experience as a practitioner was central to the development of the project
My project was developed in response to previous research reports
I designed the strategy to collect information
I reapplied the strategy of another research project
I received both a resource and a strategy to collect information on its implementation
Other . . .

B. Data collection
I used information that I usually collect as part of my professional practice
I used statistical data collected by the school and/or department
I used departmental and/or site records
I used secondary sources such as departmental statistics
I collected published documents
I distributed a survey
I used a pretest and posttest approach
I was observed and/or recorded in my practice
I recorded observations of my students
I was interviewed
I conducted interviews
I kept a journal of creative and/or reflective writing
I collected artifacts
I recorded responses to objects and/or audiovisual texts
I made a case study of a small number of students
I recorded classroom discussion and student–teacher interaction
Other . . .

C. Analysis
I drew from my impressions formed during the inquiry
I used statistical measures
I used a checklist of teaching practices
I compared data to curriculum outcomes and/or standardized tests
I selected data around a predetermined theme/focus
I found common words and phrases used
I identified repeated themes and/or situations
I focused on unique statements and/or events
I involved my students in analyzing the data
I involved my colleagues in analyzing the data
I did not have the opportunity to complete the analysis stage
Other . . .

D. Reporting
I have told others about my research findings
I presented the findings of my research to my school colleagues
I wrote a research report for my employer
I wrote a report for the university research team
I presented my research findings at a seminar/conference
I wrote a thesis for university accreditation
The findings of my research were published on the Internet
I was interviewed by the media about my research project
Other . . .

SECTION C—IMPACTS

This section asks you to consider the effects that your involvement in practitioner inquiry has had, first on your professional practice, and then on your career trajectory.

- By *professional practice*, we mean the things you do as part of your role as an educator or educational leader—what you do that makes up your work. We have split the impacts into subcategories so that you consider: impacts on how you view your practice, the practices that have been impacted, impacts on resources you use, and impacts on the school or beyond.

- By *career trajectory*, we mean the various roles that you have taken on over the past 10 years that may have taken you beyond the classroom or been combined with working in classrooms.

5. Impacts You Have Experienced on Your *Professional Practice*

Please select from the lists below to indicate the impacts you have experienced as a result of your involvement in inquiry projects. Tick as many impacts as apply to you, and add any other impacts not listed.

A. How I *view* my practice
I experienced minimal or no impact on how I view my practice
I view my students differently (e.g., I look for strengths, I am more aware of learning difficulties, I think about what students are bringing to school from home and/or the community)
I view classroom interactions differently (e.g., between students, between myself and students)
I view the curriculum differently (e.g., I notice the different opportunities curriculum offers students, I see possibilities for modifying the curriculum)
I see so many problems that it is sometimes overwhelming
I see connections between my practice and educational theories/research
Other . . .

B. My teaching practices
I have discovered a specific activity or approach that is particularly effective and that I have continued to use
I have increased the diversity of learning activities I offer to students
I have increased the range of assessment approaches I use
I experienced minimal or no impact on my teaching practice
I have integrated inquiry practices into my teaching (e.g., I undertake focused observations, I systematically analyze student data)
I have been unable to integrate inquiry practices into my teaching (owing to insufficient time, lack of support, and so on)
I have ceased a particular activity or approach that I now do not believe is effective/appropriate
Although during my inquiry I experienced new practices, I decided it was better/more practical to maintain my usual approach
I have incorporated more opportunities for students to make choices about how they learn
Other . . .

C. The resources I use for teaching
I have modified existing resources so that they are more appropriate for my students
I have developed new resources
I have stopped using certain resources
I have not been able to find appropriate resources to put into place the new practices I would like to undertake
I make greater use of community resources (e.g., through inviting local people to share their knowledge, by visiting local places)
I make more use of ICTs for learning
I experienced minimal or no impact on the resources I use for teaching
Other . . .

D. School- or system-level policies and practices
My inquiry contributed to the adoption of new teaching practices by colleagues at my school and/or within a network of schools
Resources generated by my inquiry activities have been taken up and used by colleagues at my school and/or within a network of schools

No changes beyond my own practice flowed from my inquiry

As a result of my inquiry, school-level policies were changed

My inquiry contributed to system-level policy change

Other . . .

6. Impacts You Have Experienced on Your *Career Trajectory*

Please select from the list below to indicate the impacts you have experienced as a result of your involvement in inquiry projects. Tick as many impacts as apply to you, and add any other impacts not listed.

A. My professional skills: As a result of my inquiry . . .

I have not added to my skills

I have developed my skills of data analysis

I have acquired new presentation skills

I have developed my professional/academic writing skills

I have acquired new skills in the use of ICTs

There has been no opportunity to use the skills I gained through my inquiry

Other . . .

B. My professional profile: Since completing my inquiry . . .

I have made a presentation(s) to professional colleagues relating to my inquiry

I have initiated and/or taken leadership of a collaborative inquiry

Some of my colleagues have been dismissive of the findings of my inquiry

I have written for publication

I was selected for a committee or working group

There has been no impact on my professional profile related to my participation in inquiry

I believe my experience in practitioner inquiry helped me gain a promotion

My experience in practitioner inquiry has encouraged me to leave the classroom

My colleagues view me as someone who is knowledgeable/skilled in inquiry and/or in the subject of my inquiry

Some of my colleagues have been critical of my inquiry activities (e.g., the time spent, the requirement of their own participation)

I have run professional development related to inquiry or to the subject of my inquiry

I received an award or other type of formal recognition related to my inquiry work

Other . . .

C. My orientation to lifelong learning: As a result of completing my inquiry . . .

I have increased my reading of professional and/or research literature

I have a greater understanding of the literature that I read

I have undertaken accredited university courses following my experience with practitioner inquiry (these courses need not be research related)

The inquiry had minimal or no impact on my orientation to lifelong learning

I have attended one or more conferences related to inquiry or to the subject of my inquiry

Other . . .

SECTION D—MOST SIGNIFICANT IMPACTS

In this section, we ask you to think about the full range of projects that you listed in Section A, and indicate which have been most significant in terms of your professional practice and your career. By *significance*, we mean which have had the greatest impact. *If you believe your participation in practitioner inquiry has had minimal or no impact, please do not complete this section.* As in Section C, we have split these questions into one about impact on professional practice and one on career trajectory.

7. Specific Impacts on Your *Professional Practice*

Thinking through the projects that you named in Section A, which of these has impacted most significantly on your professional practice?

Project   *(please circle)*   1   2   3   4   5

In what ways was your practice impacted on by this project?

What was it about this project that contributed to this impact?

8. Specific Impacts on Your *Career Trajectory*

Thinking through the projects that you named in Section A, which of these has impacted most significantly on your career trajectory?

Project   *(please circle)*   1   2   3   4   5

In what ways was your career impacted on by this project?

What was it about this project that contributed to this impact?

SECTION E—STATISTICAL INFORMATION

Your completion of this section will help us consider how practitioner inquiry has impacted people in different places, positions, and stages of their career. We also ask about any academic study you've done that has involved practitioner inquiry. Finally, we ask if you are willing to be contacted by us for a follow-up interview to explore issues that can't be taken up in such a short survey.

9. Current Status

Please supply the details below for our records.

Gender:

School:

Current position:

Years of teaching experience:

10. Academic Programs Involving Practitioner Inquiry

Please indicate any academic programs undertaken that have involved a component of practitioner inquiry.

Program type: (please circle)	Institution: (please indicate whether UniSA or other)
Graduate certificate	
Master's	
Doctorate	

11. Further Involvement

Are you willing to participate in an interview about your involvement in practitioner inquiry projects? If you are willing to be interviewed, please provide your name and contact information.

Yes   No

Name: _____

Contact number: _____

Thank you for completing this survey.

References

Abell, S., Smith, D. C., & Volkmann, M. (2006). Inquiry in science teacher education. In I. Flick & N. Lederman (Eds.), *Scientific inquiry and the nature of science: Implications for teaching, learning and teacher education* (pp. 173–199). Dordrecht, Netherlands: Springer.

Alloway, N., Freebody, P., Gilbert, P., & Muspratt, S. (2002). *Boys, literacy and schooling: Expanding the repertoires of practice*. Canberra, Australia: Commonwealth of Australia.

Altrichter, H., Posch, P., & Somekh, B. (1993). *Teachers investigate their work: An introduction to the methods of action research*. London, England: Routledge.

Amery, R. (2014, August). *The diaspora returns: The crystallisation of a Kaurna linguistic identity*. Paper presented at the Research Centre for Languages and Cultures Symposium, Adelaide, Australia.

Anagnostopoulos, D., Sykes, G., McCrory, R., Cannata, M., & Frank, K. (2010). Dollars, distinction, or duty? The meaning of the National Board for Professional Teaching Standards for teachers' work and collegial relations. *American Journal of Education, 116*(3), 337–369.

Anderson, G., & Herr, K. (2011). Scaling up "evidence-based" practices for teachers is a profitable but discredited paradigm. *Educational Researcher, 40*(6), 287–289.

Armstrong, F., & Moore, M. (2004). Action research: Developing inclusive practice and transforming cultures. In F. Armstrong & M. Moore (Eds.), *Action Research for Inclusive Education* (pp. 1–16). London, England: Taylor and Francis.

Armstrong, T. (2001). IKSWAL: Interesting Kids Saddled with Alienating Labels. *Educational Leadership, 59*(3), 38–41.

Attard, K. (2007). Habitual practice vs. the struggle for change: Can informal teacher learning promote ongoing change to professional practice? *International Studies in Sociology of Education, 17*(1), 147–162.

Au, K. (1997). Ownership, literacy achievement, and students of diverse cultural backgrounds. In J. G. A. Wigfield (Ed.), *Reading Engagement: Motivating readers through integrated instruction* (pp. 168–182). Newark: International Reading Association.

Australian Institute for Teaching and School Leadership (AITSL). (2011). *National professional standards for teachers*. Canberra, Australia: Education Services of Australia.

Baker-Doyle, K. (2011). *The networked teacher: How new teachers build social networks for professional support*. New York, NY: Teachers College Press.

Bakhtin, M. M. (1981). Discourse in the novel (C. Emerson & M. Holquist, Trans.). In M. Holquist (Ed.), *The dialogic imagination: Four essays by M. M. Bakhtin* (pp. 259–422). Austin, TX: University of Texas Press.

Bakhtin, M. M. (1990). *Art and answerability: Early philosophical essays* (V. Liapunov, Trans.). Austin, TX: University of Texas Press.

Ball, S. J. (2006). *Education policy and social class: The selected works of Stephen J. Ball.* Abingdon, England: Routledge.

Balta, V. (2002, October 25). End creative teaching, official says. *Stockton Record.* Retrieved from www.recordnet.com/daily/news/articles/102502-gn-2.php

Benjamin, S. (2001). Challenging masculinities: Disability and achievement in testing times. *Gender and Education, 13*(1), 39–55.

Benjamin, S. (2002). *The micropolitics of inclusive education: An ethnography.* Buckingham, England: Open University Press.

Bennett, A., & Elman, C. (2006). Qualitative research: Recent developments in case study methods. *Annual Review of Political Science, 9*(1), 455–476.

Berger, J. G., Boles, K. C., & Troen, V. (2005). Teacher research and school change: Paradoxes, problems, and possibilities. *Teaching and Teacher Education, 21*(1), 93–105.

Berthoff, A. (1981). *The making of meaning.* Upper Montclair, NJ: Boynton Cook.

Bessant, J. (2011). Conservatives, politics and the crisis of modern education in Australia. *Policy Studies, 32*(6), 631–647.

Boomer, G. (1985). *Fair Dinkum teaching and learning: Reflections on literacy and power.* Upper Montclair, NJ: Boynton Cook.

Boomer, G., Lester, N., Onore, C., & Cook, J. (Eds.). (1992). *Negotiating the curriculum: Educating for the 21st century.* London, England: Falmer Press.

Booth, T., & Ainscow, M. (2000). *Index for inclusion: Developing learning and participation in schools.* Bristol, England: Centre for Studies in Inclusive Education.

Boulter, C. (2010). *On the periphery: Classroom teacher accounts of including special needs students in Nova Scotia* (Unpublished doctoral dissertation). University of South Australia, Adelaide, Australia.

Brand, M. (2009). Exhausted from educational reform. *Bulletin of the Council for Research in Music Education, 180*(Spring), 87–92.

Broderick, A. A., Hawkins, G., Henze, S., Mirasol-Spath, C., Pollack-Berkovits, R., Clune, H., Skovera, E., & Steel, C. (2012). Teacher counternarratives: Transgressing and "restorying" disability in education. *International Journal of Inclusive Education, 16*(8), 825–842.

Burns, D. (2007). *Systemic action research.* Bristol, England: Policy Press.

Bushweller, K. (1995). Turning our backs on boys. *The Education Digest, 60*(5), 9–12.

Bybee, R. (2006). Scientific inquiry and science teaching. In I. F. N. Lederman (Ed.), *Scientific inquiry and the nature of science* (pp. 1–14). Dordrecht, Netherlands: Springer.

Cameron, M., & Lovett, S. (2015). Sustaining the commitment and realising the potential of highly promising teachers. *Teachers and Teaching, 21*(2), 150–163.

Centre for Study of Policies and Practices in Education (CEPPE), Chile. (2013). Learning standards, teaching standards and standards for school principals: A comparative study. *OECD Education Working Papers, No. 99.* OECD Publishing. Retrieved from dx.doi.org/10.1787/5k3tsjqtp90v-en

Charlton, K. (2007). A bridge to history: Authentic literacy partnership in a local environment. In B. Comber, H. Nixon, & J.-A. Reid (Eds.), *Literacies in place: Teaching environmental communications* (pp. 66–81). Newtown, NSW, Australia: Primary English Teaching Association.

Clark, P. G., Moore, K. C., & Carlson, M. P. (2008). Documenting the emergence of "speaking with meaning" as a sociomathematical norm in professional learning community discourse. *Journal of Mathematical Behavior, 27*(4), 297–310.

Coburn, C. (2005). The role of nonsystem actors in the relationship between policy and practice: The case of reading instruction in California. *Educational Evaluation and Policy Analysis, 27*(1), 23–52.

Cochran-Smith, M., & Lytle, S. (1990). Research on teaching and teacher research: The issues that divide. *Educational Researcher, 19*(2), 2–11.

Cochran-Smith, M., & Lytle, S. (1993). *Inside/Outside: Teacher research and knowledge*. New York: Teachers College Press.

Cochran-Smith, M., & Lytle, S. (1999). The teacher research movement: A decade later. *Educational Researcher, 28*(7), 15–25.

Cohen, D. K. (2005). Professions of human improvement: Predicaments of teaching. In M. Nisan & O. Schremer (Eds.), *Educational Deliberations* (pp. 278–294). Jerusalem, Israel: Keter Publishers.

Comber, B. (2013). Teachers as researchers: A "fair dinkum" learning legacy. *English in Australia, 48*(3), 54–61.

Comber, B., Nixon, H., Ashmore, L., Loo, S., & Cook, J. (2006). Urban renewal from the inside out: Spatial and critical literacies in a low socioeconomic school community. *Mind, Culture and Activity, 13*(3), 228–246.

Comber, B., Nixon, H., & Reid, J.-A. (Eds.). (2007). *Literacies in place: Teaching environmental communications*. Newtown, NSW, Australia: Primary English Teaching Association.

Cormack, P. (2011). Reading pedagogy, "evidence" and education policy: Learning from history? *Australian Educational Researcher, 38*(2), 133–148.

Cormack, P., Green, B., & Nixon, H. (2007). Introduction: Literacy, place, environment. *The Australian Journal of Language and Literacy, 30*(2), 77–81.

Creswell, J. W. (2014). *Research design: Qualitative, quantitative, and mixed methods approaches* (4th ed.). Los Angeles, CA: Sage.

Cunningham, J. (2001). The National Reading Panel report. *Reading Research Quarterly, 36*(3), 326–335.

Danforth, S., & Jones, P. (2015). From special education to integration to genuine inclusion. In *Foundations of Inclusive Education Research*. Bingley, England: Emerald Group Publishing.

Darling-Hammond, L., & Richardson, N. (2009). Teacher learning: What matters? *Educational Leadership, 66*(5), 46–53.

Dawson, M. (2011). Becoming a teacher leader: Teachers re-thinking their roles. *Leading & Managing, 17*(1), 16–27.

DeBoer, G. (2006). Historical perspectives on inquiry teaching in schools. In I. Flick & N. Lederman (Eds.), *Scientific inquiry and the nature of science* (pp. 17–35). Dordrecht, Netherlands: Springer.

Diniz, F. A., & Usmani, K. (2001). Changing the discourse on race and special educational needs. *Multicultural Teaching, 20*(1), 25–28.

Dudu, W. T., & Vhurumuku, E. (2012). Teachers' practices of inquiry when teaching investigations: A case study. *Journal of Science Teacher Education, 23*(6), 579–600.

Dutschke, A. (2013). Place-based literacies in children's services. Unpublished student assignment, University of South Australia.

Edmondson, J. (2001). Prairie town: Rural life and literacies. *Journal of Research in Rural Education, 17*(1), 3–11.

Edwards, A., & Talbot, R. (2014). *The hard-pressed researcher: A research handbook for the caring professions* (2nd ed.). New York, NY: Routledge.

Elliott, J. (1978). What is action research in schools? *Journal of Curriculum Studies, 10*(4), 355–357.

Engvik, G. (2014). The importance of networks for newly qualified teachers in upper secondary education. *Educational Researcher, 56*(4), 453–472.

Everitt, J. G. (2012). Teacher careers and inhabited institutions: Sense-making and arsenals of teaching practice in educational institutions. *Symbolic Interaction, 35*(2), 203–220.

Fish, D. (2009). Research as pragmatic practice: Unpredictable means, unforeseeable ends. In B. Green (Ed.), *Understanding and researching professional practice* (pp. 135–151). Rotterdam, Netherlands/Taipei, Taiwan: Sense Publishers.

Fisher, K. (2005). *Dimensions of diversity case study*. Unpublished manuscript.

Freeman, D. (1993). Renaming experience/reconstructing practice: Developing new understandings of teaching. *Teaching & Teacher Education, 9*(5/6), 485–497.

Freeman, D. (1998). *Doing teacher-research: From inquiry to understanding*. Pacific Grove, CA: Heinle and Heinle.

Fullan, M. (2001). *The new meaning of educational change*. London, England: Routledge.

Fullan, M. (2004). *Leadership and sustainability*. Paper presented at the Hot Seat Seminar, Urban Leadership Community, United Kingdom.

Fullan, M. (2006). The future of educational change: System thinkers in action. *Journal of Educational Change, 7*, 113–122.

Gee, J. (1990). *Social linguistics and literacies: Ideology in discourses*. New York & Philadelphia: Falmer.

Giroux, H. (1998). *Channel surfing: Racism, the media and the destruction of today's youth*. New York, NY: St. Martin's Press.

Goswami, D., & Stillman, P. (1987). *Reclaiming the classroom: Teacher research as an agency for change*. Upper Montclair, NJ: Boynton Cook.

Gray, J., & Myers, M. (1978). The Bay Area Writing Project. *The Phi Delta Kappan, 59*(6), 410–413.

Green, B. (Ed.) (1999). *Designs on learning: Essays on curriculum and teaching by Garth Boomer*. Canberra, Australia: Australian Curriculum Studies Association.

Green, B. (2009). *Understanding and researching professional practice*. Rotterdam, Netherlands: Sense Publishers.

Griffiths, M. (1998). *Educational research for social justice: Getting off the fence*. Buckingham, England: Open University Press.

Groundwater-Smith, S., Mitchell, J., & Mockler, N. (2016). Praxis and the language of improvement: Inquiry based approaches to authentic improvement in Australasian schools. *School Effectiveness and School Improvement, 27*(1), 80–90.

Guttierez, K. D., & Penuel, W. (2014). Relevance of practice as a criterion for rigor. *Educational Researcher, 43*(1), 19–23.

Halliday, M. (1978). *Language as social semiotic: The social interpretation of language and meaning.* London, England: Edward Arnold.

Hamilton, D. (2005). Knowing practice. *Pedagogy, Culture & Society, 13*(2), 285–289.

Handsfield, L., Crumpler, T., & Dean, T. (2010). Tactical negotiations and creative adaptations: The discursive production of literacy curriculum and teacher identities across space-times. *Reading Research Quarterly, 45*(4), 405.

Hargreaves, D. H. (1999). The knowledge-creating school. *British Journal of Educational Studies, 47*(2), 122–144.

Hashweh, M. (2004). Case-writing as border-crossing: Describing, explaining and promoting teacher change. *Teachers and Teaching: Theory and Practice, 10*(3), 229–246.

Heath, S. B. (1983). *Ways with words: Language, life, and work in communities and classrooms.* Cambridge, England: Cambridge University Press.

Hicks, D. (2002). *Reading lives: Working-class children and literacy learning.* New York, NY: Teachers College Press.

Horvat, E., Weininger, E., & Lareau, A. (2003). From social ties to social capital: Class differences in the relations between schools and parent networks. *American Educational Research Journal, 40*(2), 319–351.

Howe, K., R. (2009). Positivist dogmas, rhetoric, and the education science question. *Educational Researcher, 38*(6), 428–440.

Howes, A., Booth, T., Dyson, A., & Frankham, J. (2005). Teacher learning and the development of inclusive practices and policies: Framing and context. *Research Papers in Education, 20*(2), 133–148.

Howes, A., Frankham, J., Ainscow, M., & Farrell, P. (2004). The action in action research: Mediating and developing inclusive intentions. *Educational Action Research, 12*(2), 239–258.

Huberman, M. (1993). The model of the independent artisan in teachers' professional relations. In J. Little & M. McLaughlin (Eds.), *Teachers' work: Individuals, colleagues and contexts* (pp. 11–50). New York, NY: Teachers College Press.

Hustler, D., McNamara, O., Jarvis, J., Londra, M., & Campbell, A. (2003). *Teachers' perceptions of continuing professional development.* Colegate, England: Department for Education and Skills.

Jackson, A. Y. (2001). Multiple Annies: Feminist poststructural theory and the making of a teacher. *Journal of Teacher Education, 52*(5), 386–397.

Janks, H. (1993). *Language identity and power.* Johannesburg, South Africa: Hodder & Stoughton.

Jones, S. (2004). Living poverty and literacy learning: Sanctioning topics of students' lives. *Language Arts, 81*(6), 461–469.

Jule, A. (2004). Speaking in silence: A case study of a Canadian Punjabi girl. In B. Norton & A. Pavlenko (Eds.), *Gender and English language learners* (pp. 69–78). Alexandria, VA: TESOL Inc.

Kemmis, S. (2005). Knowing practice: Searching for salience. *Pedagogy, Culture & Society, 13*(2), 391–426.

Kemmis, S. (2006). Participatory action research and the public sphere. *Educational Action Research, 14*(4), 459–476.

Kemmis, S. (2009). Understanding professional practice: A synoptic framework. In B. Green (Ed.), *Understanding and researching professional practice*. Rotterdam, Netherlands: Sense Publishers.

Kemmis, S. (2010). What is to be done? The place of action research. *Educational Action Research, 18*(4), 417–427.

Kemmis, S. (2011). Researching educational praxis: Spectator and participant perspectives. *British Educational Research Journal, 38*(6), 885–905.

Kemmis, S., McTaggart, R., & Nixon, R. (2014). *The action research planner: Doing critical participatory action research*. Singapore: Springer.

Kerkham, L., & Comber, B. (2007). Literacy, places and identity: The complexity of teaching environmental communications. *Australian Journal of Language and Literacy, 30*(2), 134–148.

Kickett-Tucker, C. (1998). *Research and urban Aboriginal school children: Considerations and implications*. Paper presented at the Australian Association for Research in Education National Conference, Adelaide, Australia.

Kim, H., & Hannafin, M. (2009). Web-enhanced case-based activity in teacher education: A case study. *Instructional Science, 37*(2), 151–170.

Kutnick, P. (2000). Girls, boys and school achievement: Critical comments on who achieves in schools and under what economic and social conditions achievement takes place—A Caribbean perspective. *International Journal of Educational Development, 20*(1), 65–84.

Labaree, D. (2008). The dysfunctional pursuit of relevance in educational research. *Educational Researcher, 37*(7), 421–423.

Lankshear, C., & Knobel, M. (2004). *A handbook for teacher research*. Thousand Oaks, CA: Sage.

Lather, P. (1991). *Getting smart: Feminist research and pedagogy with/in the postmodern*. New York, NY: Routledge.

Latta, M. M., & Kim, J.-H. (2010). Narrative inquiry invites professional development: Educators claim the creative space of praxis. *The Journal of Educational Research, 103*(3), 137–148.

Lawn, M. (1999). Designing teaching: The classroom as a technology. In I. Grosvenor, M. Lawn, & K. Rousmaniere (Eds.), *Silences and images: The social history of the classroom* (pp. 63–83). New York, NY: Peter Lang.

Le Fevre, D. (2014). Barriers to implementing pedagogical change: The role of teachers' perceptions of risk. *Teaching and Teacher Education, 38*, 56–64.

Lemke, J. (1990). *Talking science: Language learning and values*. Norwood, NJ: Ablex.

Lewis, C. (2015). What is improvement science? Do we need it in education? *Educational Researcher, 44*(1), 54–61.

Liew, W. M. (2012). Perform or else: The performative enhancement of teacher professionalism. *Asia Pacific Journal of Education, 32*(3), 285–303.

Light, P., & Littleton, K. (1999) *Social processes in children's learning*. Oxford, England: Oxford University Press.

Lingard, B., Martino, W., Mills, M., & Bahr, M. (2002). *Addressing the educational needs of boys: Strategies for schools and teachers*. Canberra, Australia: Commonwealth of Australia.

Lytle, S., & Cochran-Smith, M. (1992). Teacher research as a way of knowing. *Harvard Educational Review, 62*(4), 447–474.

McInerney, P. (2005). Counting and accounting for social justice in the devolved school: How do indigenous students fare? *Melbourne Studies in Education, 46*(1), 13–32.

Mackey, J., & Evans, T. (2011). Interconnecting networks of practice for professional learning. *International Review of Research in Open and Distance Learning, 12*(3), 1– 17.

Malaguzzi, L. (1993). *Your image of the child: Where teaching begins. Exchange, 94*(3), 1–5.

Marsh, A. (2013). Pomberuk-angk. Nganawi pulgi. Murray Bridge my place. Unpublished student assignment, University of South Australia.

Marshall, J., Horton, R., Igo, B., & Switzer, D. (2009). K–12 science and mathematics teachers' beliefs about and use of inquiry in the classroom. *International Journal of Science and Mathematics Education, 7*, 575–596.

McLaughlin, M., & O'Brien-Strain, M. (2008). The youth data archive: Integrating data to assess social settings in a societal sector framework. In M. Shin & H. Yoshikawa (Eds.), *Toward positive youth development: Transforming schools and community programs* (pp. 313–332). Oxford, England: Oxford University Press.

McWilliam, E. (2004). W(h)ither practitioner research? *Australian Educational Researcher, 31*(2), 113–126.

McWilliam, E., & Singh, P. (2004). Safety in numbers? Teacher collegiality in the risk-conscious school. *Journal of Educational Enquiry, 5*(1), 22–33.

Meredith, C. (2006). Children's voice on integrated peer play opportunities. Unpublished student assignment, University of South Australia.

Miller, L. (2005). Redefining teachers, reculturing schools: Connections, commitments and challenges. In A. Hargreaves (Ed.), *Extending educational change: International handbook of educational change*. Dordrecht, Netherlands: Springer.

Miller Marsh, M. (2002). Examining the discourses that shape our teacher identities. *The Ontario Institute for Studies in Education, 32*(4), 453–469.

Moll, L. C. (1990). Literacy research in community and classrooms: A sociocultural approach. In K. Beach (Ed.), *Multidisciplinary perspectives in literacy*. Urbana, IL: National Conference in Research on English.

Neuman, S., & Celano, D. (2006). The knowledge gap: Implications of leveling the playing field for low-income and middle-income children. *Reading Research Quarterly, 41*(2), 176–201.

Nichols, S. (2003). Reading the social world. In J. Barnett & B. Comber (Eds.), *Look again: Longitudinal case studies of children learning literacy* (pp. 85–98). Rozelle, NSW, Australia: Primary English Teaching Association.

Nichols, S., & Cormack, P. (2009). Making boys at home in school: Theorising and researching literacy (dis)connections. *English in Australia, 44*(3).

Nichols, S. & Nixon, H. (2013) Space, place and early childhood literacy. In J. Larson & J. Marsh (Eds.), *Handbook of early childhood literacy* (pp. 279–294). London, England: Sage.

Nind, M., & Thomas, G. (2005). Reinstating the value of teachers' tacit knowledge for the benefit of learners: Using "Intensive Interaction." *Journal of Research in Special Educational Needs, 5*(3), 97–100.

Nixon, H., Comber, B., & Cormack, P. (2007). River literacies: Researching in contradictory spaces of cross-disciplinarity and normativity. *English Teaching: Practice and Critique, 6*(3), 92–111.

Noack, A., & Schmidt, T. (2013). Narrating networks: A narrative approach of relational data collection. *Procedia Social and Behavioral Sciences, 100*, 80–93.

Noffke, S. (2008). Research relevancy or research for change. *Educational Researcher, 37*(7), 429–431.

Noffke, S., & Stevenson, R. (Eds.). (1995). *Educational action research: Becoming practically critical.* New York, NY: Teachers College Press.

O'Day, J. (2002). Complexity, accountability, and school improvement. *Harvard Educational Review, 72*(3), 293–329.

Oliver, M. (1990). *The politics of disablement.* Basingstoke, England: Macmillan.

Oliver, M. (2013). The social model of disability: Thirty years on. *Disability & Society, 28*(7), 1024–1026.

Oppong-Nuako, J., Shore, B. M., Saunders-Stewart, K. S., & Gyles, P. D. T. (2015). Using brief teacher interviews to assess the extent of inquiry in classrooms. *Journal of Advanced Academics, 26*(3), 197–226.

Owen, S. (2014). Teacher professional learning communities: Going beyond contrived collegiality toward challenging debate and collegial learning and professional growth. *Australian Journal of Adult Learning, 54*(2), 54–78.

Owens, D. (2010). Commercial reading programmes as the solution to children living in poverty. *Literacy, 44*(3), 112–121.

Peshkin, A. (2000). The nature of interpretation in qualitative research. *Educational Researcher, 29*(9), 5–9.

Poetter, T. S., Badiali, B., & Hammond, D. J. (2000). Growing teacher inquiry: Collaboration in a partner school. *Peabody Journal of Education, 75*(3), 161–175.

Prochner, L., Cleghorn, A., & Green, N. (2008). Space considerations: Materials in the learning environment in three majority world preschool settings. *International Journal of Early Years Education, 16*(3), 189–201.

Purdue, K., Ballard, K., & MacArthur, J. (2001). Exclusion and inclusion in New Zealand early childhood education: Disability, discourses and contexts. *International Journal of Early Years Education, 9*(1), 37–49.

Ramnarain, U. D. (2013). Teachers' perceptions of inquiry-based learning in urban, suburban, township and rural high schools: The context-specificity of science curriculum implementation in South Africa. *Teaching and Teacher Education, 38*, 65–75.

Reid, J.-A., & Green, B. (2009). Researching (from) the standpoint of the practitioner. In B. Green (Ed.), *Understanding and researching professional practice* (pp. 165–184). Rotterdam, Netherlands/Taipei, Taiwan: Sense Publishers.

Reid, R., Maag, J., & Vasa, S. (1993). Attention deficit hyperactivity disorder as a disability category: A critique. *Exceptional Children, 60*(3), 198–214.

Reilly, M. A. (2009). Dressing the corpse: Professional development and the play of singularities. *Journal of Curriculum and Pedagogy, 6*(1), 79–99.

Riecken, T., Conibear, F., Michel, C., Lyall, J., Scott, T., Tanaka, M., Stewart, S., Riecken, J., & Strong-Wilson, T. (2006). Resistance through re-presenting culture: Aboriginal filmmakers and a participatory action research. *Canadian Journal of Education, 29*(1), 265–286.

Riveros, A., Newton, P., & Burgess, D. (2012). A situated account of teacher agency and learning: Critical reflections on professional learning communities. *Canadian Journal of Education, 35*(1), 202–216.

Salmon, G. (2002). *E-tivities: The key to active online learning*. London, England: Kogan Page.

Santrock, J. (2007). *Child development* (11th ed.). Boston, MA: McGraw-Hill.

Schechter, C. (2012). Developing teachers' collective learning: Collective learning from success as perceived by three echelons in the school system. *International Journal of Educational Research, 56*, 60–74.

Schön, D. (1983). *The reflective practitioner: How professionals think in action*. San Francisco, CA: Jossey-Bass.

Schreurs, B. (2014). Analysing learning ties to stimulate continuous professional development in the workplace. In V. Hodgson (Ed.), *The design, experience and practice of networked learning* (pp. 207–224). Heerlen, Netherlands: Springer.

Selkriga, M., & Keamya, K. (2014). Promoting a willingness to wonder: Moving from congenial to collegial conversations that encourage deep and critical reflection for teacher educators. *Teachers and Teaching: Theory and Practice, 21*(4), 421–236.

Sellar, S., & Cormack, P. (2009). Redesigning pedagogies in middle years: Challenges for teachers working with disadvantaged students. *Pedagogy, Culture and Society, 17*(2), 123–139.

Singh, P. (2001). Speaking about cultural difference and school disadvantage: An interview study of "Samoan" paraprofessionals in designated disadvantaged secondary schools in Australia. *British Journal of Sociology of Education, 22*(3), 317–337.

Skilbeck, M. (1983). Lawrence Stenhouse: Research methodology. *British Educational Research Journal, 9*(1), 11–20.

Slattery, L. (2003, May 21). It's a bloke thing. *The Australian*, p. 9.

Smith, D. E. (1990). *Texts, facts and femininity: Exploring relations of ruling*. London, England: Routledge.

Smith, D. E. (1999). *Writing the social: Critique, theory and investigations*. Toronto, Canada: University of Toronto Press.

Smith, D. E. (2005). *Institutional ethnography: A sociology for people*. Lanham, MD: Altamira Press.

Snyder, S. (2013). The simple, the complicated, and the complex: Educational reform through the lens of complexity theory. *OECD Education Working Papers*. OECD. Retrieved from dx.doi.org/10.1787/5k3txnpt1lnr-en

Song, M., & Miskel, C. (2005). Who are the influentials? A cross-state social network analysis of the reading policy domain. *Educational Administration Quarterly, 41*(1), 7–48.

Stacey, R. D. (1995). The science of complexity: An alternative perspective for strategic change processes. *Strategic Management Journal, 16*(6), 477–495.

Stenhouse, L. (1975). *An introduction to curriculum research and development*. London, England: Heinemann.

Stenhouse, L. (1985). *Research as a basis for teaching: Readings from the work of Lawrence Stenhouse*. London, England: Heinemann.

Sun, M., Penuel, W., Frank, K., Gallagher, H. A., & Youngs, P. (2013). Shaping professional development to promote the diffusion of instructional expertise among teachers. *Educational Evaluation and Policy Analysis, 35*(3), 344–369.

Taylor, P. (2015). Learning about professional growth through listening to teachers. *Professional Development in Education, 41*(1), 1–19.

Thompson, P. (2008). The anatomy of a teachable moment: Implications for teacher educators. *Journal of Inquiry & Action in Education, 1*(2), 19–33.

Thomson, P., Hall, C., & Jones, K. (2013). Towards educational change leadership as a discursive practice—or should all school leaders read Foucault? *International Journal of Leadership in Education, 16*(2), 155–172.

Titchkosky, T. (2007). *Reading and writing disability differently: The textured life of embodiment.* Toronto, Canada: University of Toronto Press.

Toope, D. (2008). *Teacher research as professional development: Investigating my practice and teachers' relations with knowledge* (Unpublished doctoral thesis). University of South Australia, Adelaide.

Van Es, E., & Sherin, M. G. (2008). Mathematics teachers' "learning to notice" in the context of a video club. *Teaching and Teacher Education, 24,* 244–276.

Vera, E., & Schupp, T. (2006). Network analysis in comparative social sciences. *Comparative Education, 42*(3), 405–429.

Voloshinov, V. N. (1986). *Marxism and the philosophy of language* (Trans. L. Matejka & I. R. Titunik). Cambridge, MA: Harvard University Press.

Weaver-Hightower, M. (2003). The "boy turn" in research on gender and education. *Review of Educational Research, 73*(4), 471–498.

Weidmann, K. (2004, November 1). The girls are turning boys into winners. *Evening Standard,* pp. 3, 4.

Welner, K., & Mathis, W. (2015, February). Reauthorization of the Elementary and Secondary Education Act: Time to move beyond test-focused policies. *NEPC Policy Memo.* Retrieved from nepc.colorado.edu/files/nepc-policymemo-esea .pdf

Wenger, E. (1998). *Communities of practice: Learning, meaning, and identity.* Cambridge, England: Cambridge University Press.

Wright, R. (2008). Kicking the habitus: Power, culture and pedagogy in the secondary school music curriculum. *Music Education Research, 10*(3), 389–402.

Younger, M., & Warrington, M. (2005). *Raising boys' achievement.* Colegate, Norwich, England: Department for Education and Skills.

Index

The letter *f* following a page number indicates a figure.

About the Authors

Sue Nichols is senior lecturer at the School of Education, University of South Australia. She began her teaching career as a secondary English educator and was inspired to work toward more-inclusive education when she took up the role of literacy coordinator in a school for excluded students. For the last 20 years she has worked at the University of South Australia as a teacher educator and researcher, often in collaboration with practitioner colleagues. Sue also authored the book *Resourcing Early Learners: New Networks, New Actors* (Routledge, 2012).

Phil Cormack is adjunct research associate professor at the Centre for Research in Education, University of South Australia. He has been an elementary and middle school teacher, a curriculum writer and consultant, and most recently a university teacher and researcher. He has been the director of the Centre for Studies in Literacy and Learning Cultures at the University of South Australia and has conducted research with teachers on curriculum, learning, and pedagogy from the early years to senior secondary schooling.